Historical Demography

through Genealogies

HISTORICAL DEMOGRAPHY THROUGH GENEALOGIES

Explorations into Pre-1900 American Population Issues

ALBERT E. MCCORMICK JR., PHD

M² RESEARCH AND CONSULTING

iUniverse, Inc.
Bloomington

Historical Demography through Genealogies
Explorations into Pre-1900 American Population Issues

iUniverse books may be ordered through booksellers or by contacting:

iUniverse
1663 Liberty Drive
Bloomington, IN 47403
www.iuniverse.com
1-800-Authors (1-800-288-4677)

ISBN: 978-1-4620-4000-1 (sc)
ISBN: 978-1-4620-4002-5 (hc)
ISBN: 978-1-4620-4001-8 (ebk)

Printed in the United States of America

iUniverse rev. date: 09/13/2011

TABLE OF CONTENTS

FIGURES AND TABLES

DEDICATION

For Patrick and Mary Kyle Black, Johann Martin and Margeretha Mansberger, John and Sarah Sloan McCormick, Frederick and Maria Elizabeth Pershing, and all of their descendants.

PREFACE

When I was a pre-teen in Pittsburgh, my aunt Janet married Dr. Clayton J. McDole and moved to Seattle, where both were employed in an aerospace corporation. Soon afterwards, my family moved to Florida, where I attended high school and undergraduate college. After earning my doctorate, I moved to Middle Georgia where I spent the entirety of my academic career. In spite of the great distance between Aunt Janet and me, we corresponded, talked from time to time on the telephone, and, very occasionally saw each other in person. She had always shared her mother's (my grandmother, Clara R. McCormick) interest in family history. As I grew older and my own curiosity in the subject increased, our correspondence and discussions centered more and more on this topic. Sometime before her death in 1994, Aunt Janet sent me genealogical works on two branches of our antecedents, the Blacks and the Manspergers. The former was compiled and privately published by Dr. Samuel Black McCormick in 1913; the latter was compiled by F.L. Mansberger and privately published in 1979 by the Mannsperger Families of America, Inc.[1] Both volumes contained handwritten updates and corrections entered by Grandma McCormick and Aunt Janet.

Dr. Samuel McCormick had an interesting and noteworthy career as an attorney turned clergyman turned academic. In reading his obituary,

---

[1] Note the variations in the spelling of Mansperger. Thumbing through the index of this genealogy, one sees Mansperger, Mansberger, Mannsperger, Mansparger, and several other versions of the surname. Such family name permutations occurred for a variety of reasons and are not at all unusual. Variations in the Pershing name (introduced below) include, among others, Pershin, Pfersching, Pfirshing, and Persian.

reference was made to some of his forebears. This led me to an article on the McCormicks in a 1908 volume entitled *A Century and a Half of Pittsburg and Her People*, which traced the patrilineage back to County Tyrone, Ireland. By this time, I had accumulated quite a store of genealogical material. By good fortune, a colleague and golfing buddy of mine, also interested in genealogy, showed me a software program specifically designed to manage such information. I acquired this software, and spent untold months entering all of my data into it. The result was a record of vital statistics for nearly 5,500 individuals.

Included in the genealogy software program is a "report" function, which can provide summaries of all sorts of interesting information, such as age at death, age at marriage, age at first and last births, etc. At this point, the sociologist in me took over. Although my actual fields of expertise, research, and publication are in the areas of deviant behavior and the sociology of law, I did have a couple of undergraduate and graduate courses in demography. I also covered the topic in both my introductory sociology and social problems courses. I therefore knew that national information for various pre-twentieth century vital statistics were hard to come by, or nonexistent. I have also had a long-standing interest in history, which was my undergraduate minor, and in social change, which was my doctoral minor. The convergence of these interests was a study, based upon the genealogical materials I then had at hand, examining fertility, age at first marriage, and mortality in the nineteenth and early twentieth centuries. In 1996, I delivered a paper on this at the annual meeting of the Georgia Sociological Association, and, to exemplify basic demographic processes, published the article in a reader I developed for my introduction to sociology courses (A. McCormick 1998).

My uncle, Dr. Richard H. McCormick, was aware of my interest in family history. In the early 1990s, he sent me a parcel containing a treasure trove of letters, photographs, and documents. A year or two before his death in 2003, Uncle Dick followed up by sending me a fourth family genealogy. This one traced the descendants of Frederick Pershing, who immigrated to America before the Revolution. The addition of this information more than doubled my original genealogical database, which now contained over 11,800 names. Given a much more robust set of records, I decided to replicate the original study. Its findings, which form the basis of Research Inquiry 1, were presented at the 2005 meeting of the Georgia Sociological Association.

While reworking pre-1900 fertility, marriage, and mortality patterns, I was struck by a number of intriguing cultural patterns which bore further investigation. The nineteenth century was dominated early on by agriculturalism. Then, even as the Industrial Revolution advanced, the latter 1800s were still heavily influenced by agrarianism. In an era when fertility was strongly valued, the first oddity I noticed was the unusually high proportion of adult women who never had children. Curiously, about one out of eight database females in this period remained childless. The social factors associated with this surprisingly high rate of infertility are explored in Research Inquiry 2.

Not only was fertility highly valued in this age, so was marriage. Nonetheless, some individuals remained unmarried throughout their lives. On the other side of the coin, a significant number of adults were married two or more times. Neither lifelong singleness nor remarriage are unusual in modern society. However, social conditions for remaining unwed and for remarrying are now very different from what they once were. These are examined in Research Inquiry 3.

National pre-1900s mortality statistics are hard to come by. One reason is probably the result of what demographic literature terms *under-enumeration*, where deaths simply were not reported and recorded. This seemed especially true in cases of infant deaths. When examining mortality tendencies, I quickly noticed the number of times in which deceased infants were never named. Often, the records did not even indicate the gender of the child. It occurred to me that both the under-enumeration and non-naming phenomena were the result of the same nineteenth century attitude toward infants. Borrowing from anthropological literature on the significance of naming rites of passage, I pursue this question in Research Inquiry 4.

My final inquiry moved from births, marriages, and deaths to the field of occupations and structural mobility. Other than the work of C. Wright Mills, there have been few empirical investigations into pre-twentieth century stratification issues. Borrowing Mills' concepts, Research Inquiry

5 examines the wane of the old middle class and the ascendance of the new, some job-related peculiarities of both, and the occupational status of women in this era.

A Final Note: Sociological Implications synthesizes the preceding chapters' findings and conclusions, and draws on anecdotal materials extracted from the genealogies that formed the database. These illustrations humanize the statistics, tables, charts, and graphs presented earlier, and place them in socio-historical context. The outcome represents an important inquiry into pre-twentieth century customs of and attitudes toward birth, marriage, death, children, occupations, and sex roles.

ACKNOWLEDGMENTS

The subject matter of this book does not comprise the standard fare of sociological inquiry. Nonetheless, all of the separate investigations that comprise this work were, at one time or another, presented at annual meetings of the Georgia Sociological Association. This organization, to which I have belonged for many, many years, has fostered (or at least tolerated) professionally motivated efforts that transcend the normalities of the discipline. While each of the presentations was well received, each received comments and critiques offered in the spirit of helpfulness and collegiality. Resulting improvements have been incorporated into revisions.

Special note must be made of one member of the GSA, Dr. Melvin Fein of Kennesaw State University. After one of my earlier presentations, Mel approached me full of enthusiasm over my discourse, and urged me to convert it into a book. At the time, I demurred, as I had only just begun exploring the various facets of the database. At the 2008 annual meeting of the GSA, after another presentation, Mel approached me again. He told me he frequently cited examples from my work in his classes and encouraged me again to put it all in book form. Having just become Managing Editor of the GSA's on-line journal, he went further and asked me to submit one of my genealogically-based works as an article. Since then, Mel has been of tremendous mentoring assistance by proffering important advice on the book publishing process. To him go many thanks.

A great debt of gratitude is owed to Edward G. Rantze, who, professionally, wears many hats: electrical engineer, inventor, business manager, pyrotechnician, animatronics specialist, and computer/software consultant, among others. Ed's knowledge of computers and software has gotten me, a complete technophobe, out of more than one technologically-related dilemma. His entirely reliable function as my personal tech support is immensely complemented by his being a great son-in-law and wonderful father to my granddaughter.

My fellow sociologist and wife, Dr. Michelle J. McCormick, has not only supported me from the beginning on this project, she has also acted as my most important proofreader and critic. Michelle has read every draft of every chapter. She has not just corrected grammar, spelling, and technical style. More importantly, she has offered insights into the data that I had plain and simple, overlooked and flat out missed. To her, many thanks and much love.

PROLOGUE:

ON THE USE OF GENEALOGIES IN DEMOGRAPHIC RESEARCH

Scope of the Research

Statistics on births, deaths, marriage, and other vital processes provide valuable insights into social structure and behavior, both past and present. Demographic trends and patterns are particularly useful in gauging the effect and extent of social change. Unfortunately, only in modern times have national demographic data been reasonably accurate and complete (Wrong 1977:9). Comprehensive information on U.S. mortality is only available since the 1900 census (T. Smith 1960:406). The government has been keeping records on age at marriage only since 1890 (McLeod 1996:A4). Accurate registration of births and deaths in all of the United States was not achieved until 1933 (Peterson 1969:497; Wrong 1977:11). While the United States has conducted a decennial national census since 1790, it is still subject to significant error (note the undercount controversy of the 1990 census).

There are avenues to nineteenth and early twentieth century demographic information. *Historical Statistics of the United States (Colonial Times to 1957)* is a useful source. A number of socio-historical demographic studies have relied upon community or state records (see Gordon 1978). The data in these and similar sources are optimal in older, more urban, and therefore more literate sections of the country. Consequently, these demographic statistics, and their derivative studies, tend to be best for

New England states and cities. The data are sparser and less reliable as one moves to more western and less urban regions of pre-1900 America.

Community and state records provide important understandings of demographic characteristics during the 1800s and early 1900s. However, given known variations in vital processes based upon differences in residence, social class, literacy, etc., place-bound data sources have their limitations. Official vital statistics in many pre-1900 governmental entities have been lost or were accidentally destroyed.[2] Further, in any number of districts, records were never or only sporadically kept. An alternative source of information is genealogical material, which can be used to cross-check the accuracy of demographic directions generalized from locational records.

The present work makes extensive use of such information to measure nineteenth and early twentieth century rates in various vital statistics, including fertility, mortality, marriage, childlessness, and occupations. Where possible, findings are compared with known demographic patterns. The results shed further light upon demographic processes as they existed before the advent of reliable national records.

The Data

Considerable genealogical information was obtained from four inter-related published sources. Jordan (1908:50-58) traced the descendants of John and Sarah Sloan McCormick from 1788 to 1907. A sketch researched by Samuel Black McCormick (1913) delineates the descendants of Patrick and Mary Kyle Black from 1792 to 1912. Mansberger (1977) followed the descendants of Johann Martin Mansberger from 1712 to 1977. The descendants of Frederick Pershing, who immigrated to the Colonies in 1749, were outlined to 1924 by Edgar J. Pershing (1924). Supplementary information was gleaned from the notes, records, and

---

[2] For example, a recent article published in a Georgia newspaper (Skinner 2010), reported that sixty-one of Georgia's 159 counties have had a courthouse fire at least once, the first recorded in 1787.

correspondence of Clara R. McCormick and Janet McCormick McDole, which are in the author's possession.[3]

Through these sources, records were obtained on nine generations of blood relatives and, when married, their spouses for a total of 11,804 individuals. Ideally, information for each individual included date of birth, marriage, and death; number, gender, and birth dates of children; occupation; and cause of death. It is from this data that the following research inquiries into historical patterns in vital processes were derived.

While a unique source of sociological information, a genealogical database is not without its limitations. In the eighteenth and nineteenth centuries, written records were often sparse and "in the early days, curiosity as to ancestors was rudimentary or quiescent" (S. B. McCormick 1913:1). Further, the family biographers were largely untrained in the requisites of scientific data collection. On many occasions, they simply did not have access to pertinent information. The only academic was Dr. McCormick and he was trained in the classics, law, and religion, not sociology, demographics, or historiography. Some errors in the data have been uncovered and corrected. Other factual errors no doubt continue to exist.

A larger problem is missing and incomplete information, happening for a variety of reasons. Often, various pieces of information, including names, were unknown and could not be obtained by family historians. There is the additional problem of under-enumeration, a difficulty biasing socio-historic statistics. Chronicles and reports often reflected *effective* rather than actual fertility because the true number of a woman's births was not necessarily recorded. Not infrequently, infants dying soon after birth were simply ignored (See Peterson 1969:496-500).[4]

---

[3]   John and Sarah Sloan McCormick are the author's fourth great-grandparents, as are Patrick and Mary Kyle Black. Johann Martin Mansberger and his first wife, Margeretha Neusche, and Frederick Pershing and his wife Maria Elizabeth Weygant, are the author's fifth great-grandparents. Clara R. McCormick and her daughter, Janet McCormick McDole, are the author's grandmother and aunt, respectively.

[4]   Not unusually, children dying at or soon after birth were never named. Rather, they were simply listed as "infant," "infant boy," or "infant girl." The high rates of nineteenth century infant mortality provide an indication

The very nature of a genealogy makes generalizations more difficult, because there are relatively few people in the early generations. Further, by focusing on select families, genealogies are inherently susceptible to biases originating from ethnicity, social class, religion, and regionality.

No source of historical information is perfect, and the database of this series of works is no exception. However, genealogies provide yet another avenue which can be used to support, supplement, or question socio-historical inquiries based upon other data sources, as well as to suggest and generate new lines of exploration. Therefore, the scope of the investigations here provides findings which add to knowledge of pre-1900 America demographic processes. These, in turn, add intriguing comprehensions of nineteenth century society and social life.

---

of that century's attitudes toward childhood and death. This phenomenon was no doubt associated with significant under-enumeration of births, particularly in the 1800s. See the discussion on under-enumeration in the section on mortality in Research Inquiry 1. The issue of infant mortality and child naming is pursued further in Research Inquiry 4.

REFERENCES

Gordon, Michael (ed.). 1978. *The American Family in Social-Historical Perspective*. New York: St. Martin's Press.

Historical Statistics of the United States (Colonial Times to 1957). 1957. Washington, D.C.: U.S. Government Printing Office.

Jordan, John W. (ed.). 1908. *A Century and a Half of Pittsburg and Her People*. Vol. III. Pittsburgh: The Lewis Publishing Company.

Mansberger, Faye Lelia. 1979. *Descendants of the Mannsbergs, 1590-1979*. Vol. III. Privately published. Mannsperger Families of America, Inc.

McCormick, Samuel Black. 1913. *Patrick and Mary Kyle Black and Their Descendants*. Pittsburgh: Privately published.

McLeod, Ramon G. 1996. "Those Wedding Bells Keep Ringing Later." San Francisco *Chronicle* (March 14).

Pershing, Edgar J. 1924. *The Pershing Family in America*. Philadelphia: George S. Ferguson Co.

Peterson, William. 1969. *Population*. Second Edition. New York: MacMillan.

Skinner, Winston. 2010. "Many Courthouses Damaged, Destroyed by Fire over the Years." Newnan *Times-Herald* (February 10).

Smith, T. Lynn. 1960. *Fundamentals of Population Study*. Chicago: J.B. Lippencott.

Wrong, Dennis H. 1977. *Population and Society*. New York: Random House.

RESEARCH INQUIRY 1:

ON NINETEENTH CENTURY FERTILITY, MARRIAGE, AND MORTALITY[1]

Introduction

Using the genealogical database described in the prologue, it was possible to investigate nineteenth century trends in fertility, marriage, and mortality. For fertility, the data yielded information on completed family size, women's ages at first and last births, and average span of procreation. For both males and females, the database permitted examination of age at first marriage and the extent of teenage marriage. Mortality investigations were able to explore average age at death, infant and child mortality tendencies, and gender life expectancy comparisons. Where possible, findings are compared with known national statistics and patterns.

Fertility

Of all fertility measures, the database was most instrumental in determining the number of children born to each woman, a statistic analogous to *completed family size*. This measure of fertility is defined as the number

---

[1]   An earlier version of this study was presented at the 2005 annual meeting of the Georgia Sociological Association as "Using Genealogies to Examine Historical Social Structures."

of children born to women ever married, aged forty-five and over. Such information on natality was available for 2,103 married females in the data pool. These figures, grouped by females' date of birth, are presented in Appendix A and charted in Figure 1-A.

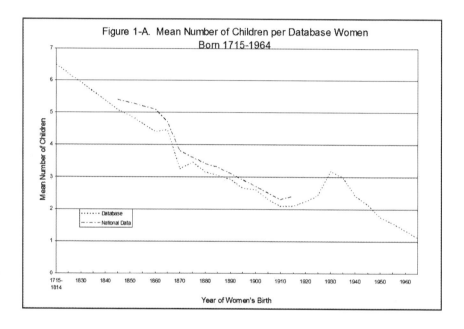

Figure 1-A. Mean Number of Children per Database Women Born 1715-1964

The findings closely parallel available national data. Not unexpectedly, the data demonstrate that fertility rates were high in the early 1800s, when women had an average of more than six children apiece. Fertility declined steadily to an average of about 4.5 children apiece for women born in the 1860s, then suddenly dropped to about two to three children per family. This drop occurred for children born, roughly, between 1900 and 1920, when the nation "made the turn" into industrialism. The drop in fertility for women born in the early 1900s and the sudden rise for women born 1915-1930 reflect the "birth dearth" of the Depression years and the post-war "baby boom," respectively.

Directions in fertility can be delineated further by observing changes in average years of childbearing. Female fecundity approximately spans from menarche in the early-to mid-teens to menopause in the mid-to late-forties. Actual fertility, of course, does not realize the potential of fecundity. The data provided age at first birth for 2,173 females, and age at last birth and average years of childbearing for 1,753 females (see Appendix B). As seen in Figure 1-B, average age at first birth has remained relatively constant over the last 200 years or so, hovering, with few exceptions, around the age of twenty-three or twenty-four. Surprisingly, this is true even during the agrarian era. Of course, some females in the data pool married and began childbearing in their teens.[2] Clearly, however, such early childbearing was the exception rather than the rule.

The finding that, since colonial times, a woman's average age at first birth has not fluctuated too wildly belies the Malthusian doctrine of delaying marriage and childbirth. Rather, the data support the Dumont-Banks model, which suggests that declining fertility rates of industrializing societies were led by the middle class (see Peterson, 1969:500-514). Instead of bearing their children later in life, as Malthus proposed, Figure 1-B shows that they ended their childbearing earlier.

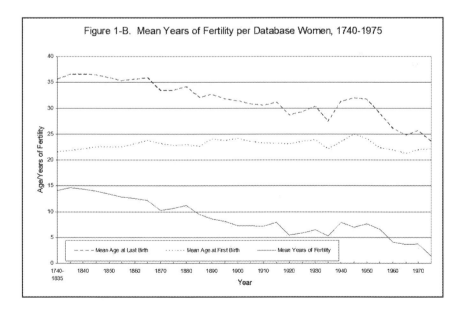

Figure 1-B. Mean Years of Fertility per Database Women, 1740-1975

---

[2]   For example, the author's fourth great-grandmother, Jane Mansberger Black, married at 15 and had the first of her fifteen children at age sixteen.

What has changed dramatically is the average age at which women ended their childbearing years and the number of years spent in having children. Until 1865-1870 women typically bore children over a span of twelve to fourteen years, and completed their families, on average, in their mid-to late 30s (and often enough for some by their early 40s). As the United States transformed into an urban industrial society, average age at last birth, average years of childbearing, and average number of births all declined. From roughly 1870 to the turn of the century, mean years spent in childbearing fell rapidly to an average of about seven years. After 1900, years devoted to childbearing continued to decline, but more slowly.

Clearly, the most important element in these findings is the age at which women ended their childbearing careers. Before the Civil War, women typically bore children into their late thirties and early forties. At the century's turn, women completed their families roughly around the age of thirty. This age dropped down into the upper twenties in the lean times of the post World War I decades, but rose into the thirties again with the "up" times of the 1940s and 1950s.

Pragmatically, then, disappearance of the large family ideal is concomitant with the advent of the twentieth century industrialism. Twentieth century fluctuations in fertility—most notably the fertility decline of the Depression, the post-war baby boom, and the birth dearth of the 1960s—are directly related to general economic conditions. The fertility declines of the nineteenth century, though, are generally explained by the demographic transition model. This paradigm posits high birth rates in agrarian cultures, in part because children are economic assets in an agricultural economy. As societies industrialize, children convert into economic liabilities, particularly to rising middle class families. The post-Civil War period is the era in which the United States clearly was transforming itself into an urban industrial society. It is in this period of time when the most dramatic nineteenth century declines in fertility occurred. By the early 1900s, the large family ideal was largely a custom of the past.

The data unmistakably demonstrate the agrarian connection with high birth rates. Table 1-A reveals husband's occupation for all women in the data pool, born before 1900, who gave birth to seven or more children.

Unfortunately, the data sources did not identify the occupational status of more than half of their husbands. Nonetheless, for those husbands whose occupations were known, the overwhelming majority were farmers. In all probability, most of those in the "unknown" category were also farm families. Not unexpectedly, women who bore seven or more children married at an earlier age (a mean age of 19.2 years), had their first child at an earlier age (mean of 21.1 years), and an extended number of childbearing years (a mean of 18.75 years).

Table 1-A. Husband's Occupational Status for Wives, Born before 1900, with Seven or More Births

Occupational Status	N	%	Mean Number of Children
Unknown	138	59.5	8.3
Farmer	73	31.5	9.3
Blue Collar	5	2.2	8.2
White-collar	7	3.0	7.7
Professional	9	3.9	8.2
Total	232	100.1	8.6

As measured by the equivalent of completed family size, the data here show a somewhat lower level of nineteenth century fertility than reported elsewhere. The discrepancies may be due to the small size of data pool age groupings, social class and rural-urban differences, and the under-enumeration exhibited by an era marked by high rates of infant mortality. Nonetheless, fertility evidenced by the women of the data pool follow expected courses. Birth rates were high at the beginning of the 1800s in a society characterized by a predominantly agricultural economy. As the effects of industrialization and urbanization were increasingly felt, fertility declined, particularly in the years following the Civil War. While women continued to *begin* their childbearing years at a relatively consistent age (early 20s), they had fewer children and completed their families at consistently younger ages (from late thirties to early thirties). As another indicator of the relative accuracy of the data, trends echo known fertility patterns of the 1900s (e.g., Depression and Baby Boom).

Age at First Marriage

In addition to Malthusian notions of delayed marriage as a "negative check" on population growth, age at marriage is a reflection of several social characteristics, including changes in educational levels, when the work force is entered, and shifts in gender roles. As detailed in Appendix C and graphed in Figure 1-C, the data sources provided information on age at first marriage for 2,409 males and 2,453 females.

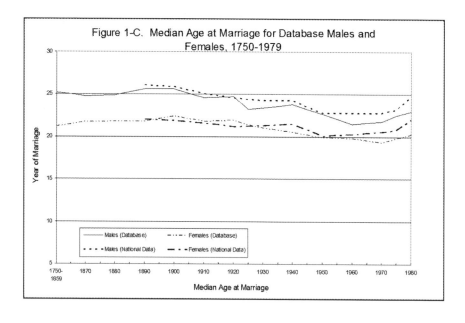

Figure 1-C. Median Age at Marriage for Database Males and Females, 1750-1979

As seen, the data for the nineteenth century rather closely parallel national data. Prior to 1900, males tended to marry, on average, in their mid-twenties (twenty-five to twenty-six). Then, around century's turn, age at marriage for males slowly dropped into the early twenties (twenty-two to twenty-three) until the 1950s. Since then, male age at marriage has increased to its current level of about twenty-five. Age at first marriage for females was relatively stable through the 1800s until the 1940s. While no doubt there were a fair share of teen marriages (as is supported by the data pool), women, on average, married around the age of twenty-two or twenty-three. Post World War II prosperity led to the 1950s' low average age of twenty. The 1960s saw women's age at first marriage moving upward, a direction which continues to the present.

Patterns in age at first marriage for both males and females doubtless represent economic conditions. In the agricultural economy of the 1800s, men might have delayed marriage until they had established farms that could financially support families (or, perhaps, could take over family farms from their fathers). Beginning in the 1900s, an urban industrial economy could provide jobs with steadier, surer, and higher incomes than those available in farming, enabling marriage at younger ages. In the present post-industrial society, because of educational requisites for the growing proportion of white-collar jobs, age at first marriage has risen. Further, the economic climate is no doubt a factor, as evidenced by marriage rates in the Great Depression and post-World War II Prosperity eras.

The economic influence on age at marriage is better seen by examining rates of teenage marriage. As presented in Appendix D, the data included 211 males and 816 females who married in their teens. Figure 1-D graphs teenage marriage from 1750 to 1979. As would be expected, far fewer males married in their teens than females. In fact, male teenage marriage was a relatively rare event until the 1900s. This gives support to the notion that males relying on farming had to be sure of their abilities to support families before entertaining the thought of marriage. Females, however, frequently married in their teens in agrarian times—until the late 1800s, more than thirty percent did. However, as agriculture waned toward the end of that century, rates of teenage female marriage declined. In point of fact, this historic period was marked generally by "hard times" on the farm, as evidenced by the several agrarian-based third-party movements of the era. With industrialization came a marked upward movement in teen female marriages. Note that both male and female marriage rates dropped noticeably during the Depression, and (concomitant with the Baby Boom) rose dramatically with the prosperous war and post-war periods.

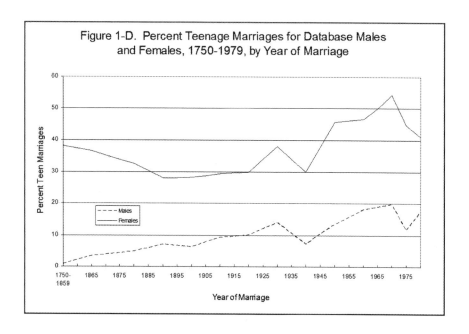

Figure 1-D. Percent Teenage Marriages for Database Males and Females, 1750-1979, by Year of Marriage

Mortality

While national data trends were not known until the 1900 census, it is clear that death rates were high in the 1800s. Consequently, as seen in Table 1-B, the study's database shows that mean ages at death were much lower than median ages at death for each time period, differences ranging from 7.7 to 12.3 years. These differences can only be explained by the high rates of infant and child mortality known to exist in the nineteenth century.

Table 1-B. Mean and Median Age at Death for Individuals Born 1800-1899			
Year of Birth	Average Length of Life		
	N	Mean Age	Median Age
1800-1849	563	58.0	66.9
1850-1869	140	52.8	60.5
1870-1884	147	50.9	61.3
1885-1899	172	49.3	61.6

The study examined rates of infant (under one year of age) and child (age one to five) mortality for 10,189 individuals in the data pool born between 1800 and 1979. This information, together with national data from 1915 onward, is provided in Appendix E and depicted in Figure 1-E.

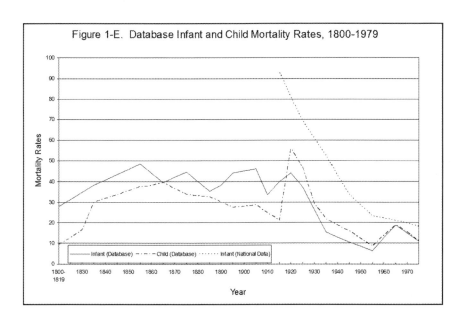

Figure 1-E. Database Infant and Child Mortality Rates, 1800-1979

Database patterns in infant and child mortality after 1915 were lower than, but generally followed the pattern of, the trends of the national data. Differences between the two sets of rates, most probably, are a function of social class differentials. However, the initial look at the pre-1900 results was disappointing. While stable, and demonstrating somewhat high rates of mortality, the findings on nineteenth century rates of infant and child mortality are unrealistically low. Estimates of infant mortality rates in colonial times range from ten to thirty percent, and it was said that until the 1900s, the typical family experienced the loss of at least one child (Vinovskis 1978). These findings, clearly, are well below such estimates.

Some of the disparity between the expected results and those actually found may very well be attributable, again, to social class differences. However, given the post-1915 differences between the original study's rates and national data, this explanation alone does not suffice. No doubt, the illiteracy rates, record-keeping practices, and the commonly incomplete records of the 1800s are contributing factors as well.

The paucity of data on infant and child deaths, though, may very well reflect an interesting social phenomenon: nineteenth century attitudes toward death and life. Peterson (1969:496-500) noted that *under-enumeration* is a not uncommon source of error in nineteenth century fertility statistics. Under-enumeration is, in essence, a measure of *effective* fertility. Actual number of births was not necessarily counted. Rather, what was reported as births were the number of children born as reduced by infant mortality. Dead infants simply were not counted as people. Corroborating this are the results of the author's study on infant mortality and child-naming (A. McCormick 2004), which comprises Research Inquiry 4 of this volume. Based on the same data pool as the current investigation, the author found evidence supporting the notion that, in agrarian America, infants were not considered full-fledged humans. In cultures with high infant death rates, the brief life of a dead child is usually just ignored.[3] Thus, it is suggested that the low rates of infant and child mortality found here are largely the result of non-reporting.

---

[3]   Two examples of known non-reporting in the present data can be given. First, the author's great-great grandmother, Rachael Black McCormick, bore seven children, two of whom did not survive child birth. One data source omitted any mention of these twins. Two other data sources acknowledged their births, but merely reported them as "twins, dying in infancy." Neither source even identified the gender of these infants. Second, the author's grandmother,

It is well known that mortality rates varied by gender. Table 1-C gives mean and median ages at death for males and females in the sample pool born between 1800 and 1899. Generally, until toward the end of the century, it seems as if males tended to outlive females. The modern tendency of females outliving males did not seem to begin until the impact of industrialism was felt.

Table 1-C. Mean and Median Age at Death for Individuals Born 1800-1899, by Gender						
Year of Birth	Average Length of Life					
	Males			Females		
	N	Mean Age	Median Age	N	Mean Age	Median Age
1800-1849	305	58.9	66.9	258	56.9	66.9
1850-1869	76	54.4	60.5	64	50.9	61.0
1870-1884	83	52.5	63.0	64	48.7	57.0
1885-1899	96	47.8	58.0	76	51.2	68.5

Examination of the age-specific mortality rates of individuals in the data pool born between 1800-1849 shows why (for data, see Appendix E). As observed in Figure 1-F, the data do not show the high rates of infant and child mortality that they should, as discussed above. However, the data clearly show that women's mortality rates were substantially higher than those of males between the ages of fifteen to forty-five, during the childbearing years. Between the ages of forty-five to sixty-five, the mortality rates of males rose more sharply than those of females and, after the age of sixty-five, gender mortality rates were virtually the same. Therefore, while life expectancy from birth favored males because of the perils of child birth, after the age of forty-five, women enjoyed a bit better life expectancy than did men.

Clara R. McCormick, bore five children. The Pershing genealogy made no mention of the fourth child, a male who died in infancy.

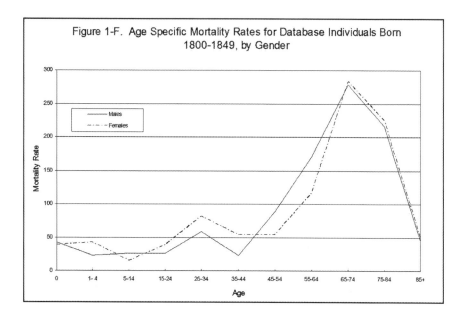

Figure 1-F. Age Specific Mortality Rates for Database Individuals Born 1800-1849, by Gender

Summary and Conclusions

As with any source of statistics for the pre-1900s, the data presented here have their limitations. Consequently, this inquiry's findings cannot be regarded as definitive. However, they can be used to confirm, add substance to, or sometimes challenge current conclusions concerning nineteenth century movements in vital processes.

The data corroborate the agricultural connection with high birth rates. As predicted by demographic transition theory, fertility steadily decreased during the 1800s. A sharp decline in birth rates occurred at the turn of the century, concomitant with accelerated rates of industrialization and urbanization. However, falling fertility was not particularly associated with changes in age at marriage. For females, median age at first marriage remained relatively unchanged until after World War II, hovering around twenty-one and a half. Further, mean age at first birth only rose from

21.5 in the early 1800s to 23.7 by 1900. Rather, the century's decline in fertility is best explained by when women *ended* their childbearing careers. By the year 1900, women were in their very early thirties, not their late thirties (or even forties), when bearing their last children. During this period of time, the mean span of childbearing years fell from 14.1 to 8.1. As industrialism further developed in the 1900s, the mean span of childbearing years continued to decline.

Industrialization and urbanization affected age at marriage for both males and females. Throughout the 1800s, males tended to be in their mid to late twenties when they married. Presumably this was because, in an agrarian-dominated economy, they needed time to acquire or establish farms capable of sustaining a family. This finding is supported by the very low rate of teen marriages among males until around the year 1900. At the end of the century, age at marriage for males dropped, and male teen marriage rates accelerated, presumably as urban jobs with dependable wages became more available. Only after World War II, when the economy shifted from an industrial to a post-industrial economy, did age at marriage for males go up. This, no doubt, has been due to the preparatory requisites for careers in an employment market increasingly emphasizing white-collar positions.

As noted above, median age at first marriage for women was relatively stable (perhaps rising slightly) all through the nineteenth century, remaining around the ages of twenty-one to twenty-two. However, female teen marriages steadily declined during the same period. Again, explanations center on the social changes accompanying the movement to an urban industrial society. For example, many males could leave the farm and directly enter into factory positions. This was not as much the case for females (at least until the time of World War II's Rosie the Riveter), especially after the passage of labor laws. Increasingly, for many urban-based women, the only jobs available were those in the lower levels of the "new" middle class created by the Industrial Revolution—stenography, clerking, sales, etc. Such positions, while not particularly remunerative, nonetheless required skills gained through completion of a high school degree. Once a job was acquired, a woman could gain a certain degree of economic independence, alleviating pressures to marry for reasons of economic security. Thus, educational requisites and financial freedom would act to delay a woman's marriage, especially teen marriage.

The data confirm high nineteenth century rates of infant and child mortality. Mortality rates were particularly significant for infants, children, and women during the childbearing years. Quite remarkably, though, the data exhibited rates of infant and child mortality well below that predicted by the literature. Social class, ethnic, urban-rural differences, etc. probably explain some of the disparity, but not all. The best explanation lies in the phenomenon of under-enumeration, where no record was made of infants who died at or soon after birth. This, in turn, reflects upon nineteenth century attitudes toward not only death, but, perhaps, toward when social life began.

In the 1800s, women had higher mortality rates between the ages of fifteen and forty-five, during the childbearing years. The explanation, of course, lies in the then contemporary perils of childbearing and child birth. Certainly, an ignorance of germ theory was a significant factor. Infectious diseases were the leading causes of death until only recently (see Peterson 1969:222-228; Wrong 1977:41-43). Specifically, it has been argued that maternal mortality was linked to then typical birthing procedures (Lipman-Blumen 1984:38-39), which elevated opportunity to contract contagious disease (particularly puerperal, or child bed fever). Other factors include lack of access to proper medical care, an inability to control undue hemorrhaging, unavailability of proper medications—in short, all of the medical technology now accessible that make pregnancy and childbirth much less traumatic.

These findings strongly suggest that nineteenth century trends in vital processes were more dynamic than usually assumed. Because of the paucity of official data from census reports or state and local statistics, research into pre-twentieth century demographic patterns in the U.S. is difficult. It is suggested that alternative data sources, such as the genealogical approach followed here, must be pursued to a much greater extent. Only then can investigators gain a more accurate picture of patterns in vital processes as they existed prior to 1900.

REFERENCES

Leslie, Gerald R. and Elizabeth M. Leslie. 1977. *Marriage in a Changing World*. New York: John Wiley and Sons.

Lipman-Blumen, Jean. 1984. *Gender Roles and Power*. Englewood Cliffs, N.J.: Prentice-Hall.

McCormick, Albert E. 2004. "Infant Mortality and Child-Naming: A Genealogical Exploration of American Trends." Presented at the annual meeting of the Georgia Sociological Association (November 13). Unicoi State Park, Georgia.

—.2005. "Using Genealogies to Examine Historical Social Structures." Presented at the annual meeting of the Georgia Sociological Association (October 22). St. Simon's Island, Georgia.

Peterson, William. 1969. *Population*. Second Edition. New York: MacMillan.

Saxton, Lloyd. 1993. *The Individual, Marriage, and the Family*. Eighth Edition. Belmont, CA: Wadsworth.

Vinovskis, Maris A. 1978. "Angel's Heads and Weeping Willows: Death in Early America." Pp. 546-563 in *The American Family in Social-Historical Perspective*, edited by Michael Gordon. New York: St. Martin's Press.

Wrong, Dennis H. 1977. *Population and Society*. New York: Random House.

RESEARCH INQUIRY 2:

ON CHILDLESSNESS
IN THE NINETEENTH CENTURY[1]

Introduction

It has long been a value, strongly held, that having children is a compelling ambition for American couples (Bell 1975:445-447). This was especially true prior to the early 1900s, when the nation, while industrializing, was still dominated by agrarian-oriented ideals. Then, as now, however, a significant minority of women remained childless by misfortune or choice (Duvall 1977:204; Winch 1963:183-185).

Reliable information on American natality is difficult to come by. Even information on childlessness in contemporary American society is rather conflictive. For today's couples, estimates range from a low of nine (Duvall 1977:204-205) to a high of twenty percent (Kephart 1972:427). Other authorities place childlessness rates somewhere in between (Bell 1975:446; Benokraitis 2005:302; Leslie and Leslie 1977:253; Saxton 1972:390; Strong, et. al. 2005:319-320).

There are several reasons for these discrepancies. Many estimates are based upon surveys targeting potentially disparate populations (national, regional, rural/urban, racial, social class, age group). Others are based

---

[1] An earlier version of this study was presented at the 2007 annual meeting of the Georgia Sociological Association as "Social Factors Related to the Infertility of Women Born between 1740-1890."

upon analysis of municipal, state, and/or federal statistics, which did not become fairly reliable until the 1950s (T. Smith 1960:284-286).

From the perspective of demography, the precision of childlessness data is important. From the perspective of sociology the *reasons* for childlessness are more of an interest. Infertility has a myriad of causes (Bell 1975:447-449; Benokraitis 2005:302-303; Kephart 1972:428; Leslie and Leslie, 1977:253; Saxton 1972:390). The origins of some childlessness are purely physical, including disabilities, reproductive disorders, hormonal imbalance, injuries, poor nutrition, illness, and disease. The bases for other instances, however, are behavioral, such as mental strain, fatigue, drug or alcohol abuse, sporadic sexual contact, and emotional stress. Probabilities of infertility increase with age, with a woman's greatest period of fecundity occurring between the ages of twenty-one and twenty-five. By the late thirties, women's fertility declined by fifty to seventy-five percent. There are even relationships between infertility and such social variables as being twice-married or being a working wife. Certainly for some, choice is the determining factor. Between five and ten percent of all married couples have decided not to have children (Bell 1975:446-447; Leslie and Leslie 1977:238; Strong, et. al.:320). Therefore, it is clear that a significant minority of American couples remain childless for sociological reasons, in spite of persistent cultural pressures.

Cultural pressures for having children were even stronger in the more agrarian culture of the nineteenth century. While vital statistics garnered in that era are often questionable, it has been estimated that childlessness in 1865-1870 was about eight percent nationally and ten percent in the northeastern states, with rates lowest in rural farm areas and highest in urban areas (Winch 1963:183-185). The immediate post-Civil War data may be anomalous, though, as estimates of infertility for the end of the century and the early 1900s rival, if not exceed, those of today (see Duvall 1977:204; Winch 1963:184).

When updating his genealogical database a few years ago, the author noticed what he deemed to be a rather significant number of married women in the 1800s who never bore a child. This was thought unusual, for though the United States was becoming an urban industrialized society during this period, agrarian-based values regarding childbirth were still strong. The present study seeks to gain perceptions into the social factors that affected this phenomenon.

Incidence of Childlessness

This study focuses on 1,460 married women in the database who were born between the years 1740 and 1890. Of these, 195 (13.4 %) were childless. Figure 2-A shows the percentage distribution of their childlessness by year of marriage. Because of the "family tree" effect, this cannot be considered a trend line. By definition, females in the earliest portion of a genealogy have borne children; their barren sisters and cousins are simply absent from the tree. Further, again by definition, there are relatively few individuals in the first few generations of any family tree. These two inter-related factors no doubt account for much of the very low rate of childlessness the figure exhibits, especially in the late 1700s and early 1800s. The actual rate of infertility was probably higher. Nonetheless, there are some noteworthy points to observe. First, Figure 1 shows a decline in childlessness during and immediately following the Civil War, which is consistent with the data presented by Winch (1963). It is believed here that this decline was a response to the horrendous casualty rate of that war, the bloodiest by far in American history. Second, Figure 1 exhibits rates in the late 1800s and early 1900s that are parallel with those estimated for contemporary society. These two observations lead to the inescapable inference that infertility in the pre-1900s era was not simply a result of classic barrenness. Rather, a variety of social factors were no doubt at play.

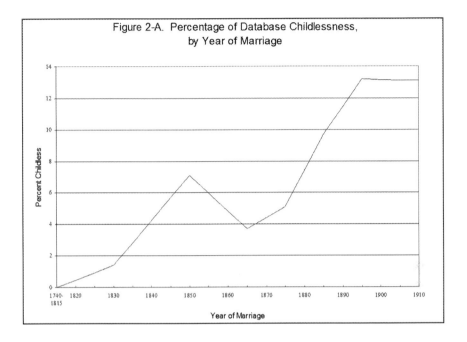

Figure 2-A. Percentage of Database Childlessness, by Year of Marriage

Social Factors and Childlessness: Findings and Discussion

Analysis of the data resulted in several intriguing findings. Factors found associated with infertility included, variously, a childless woman's age at marriage, the age difference between her and her husband, death during childbearing years, and marriage into an existing family. Table 2-A summarizes the data for childless women, where their age at marriage was known. Clearly, as a category, childless women were significantly older than the typical age at marriage for other females of the era. Between 1740 and 1910, median age at marriage for women in the entire data pool was (depending upon the decade) between 21.2 and 22.4. Median age at marriage for childless women, on the other hand, was twenty-seven and a half. Indeed, more than a third (35.9%) were age thirty or older when

19

they married. This finding is absolutely consistent with the literature cited above. Most childless women in the study did not marry at the age of highest potential fertility, the early twenties. Many, in fact, by marrying in their thirties, were in ages of significantly lower potential fertility, with far fewer years of that potential remaining. Further, for many of these childless women, the age difference between themselves and their husbands was well beyond the norm. The data pool norm for the 1740-1910 period, again depending upon the decade, was an age difference of three to four years.

Table 2-A. Age at Marriage for Database Childless Women, 1740-1910	
Median age, data pool	21.2 – 22.4
Median age, childless women (N = 192)	27.5
Childless women 30 + at marriage	69 (35.9%)

As shown in Table 2-B, however, almost thirty percent of childless wives were younger than their husbands by six years or more (where the age difference was known). About one in seven was at least ten years younger than her husband. Given that their median age at marriage was about twenty-seven and a half, this means that many childless women were marrying men who were in their mid-to late thirties, or even older.

Table 2-B. Age Difference between Database Childless Women and Their Husbands, 1740-1910 (N = 185)				
	N	%	Median age difference	Median age of wife at marriage
Wives 6 years or more younger	53	28.6%	10.5	27.6
Wives 10 years or more younger	28	15.1%	13.5	27.7
Wives 9 years or older	6	3.2%	14.5	40.0

Surprisingly, a small number of childless women married men who were significantly *younger* than they were. Six women (3.2%) married husbands who were, on average, fourteen and a half years younger. Further, at 40.0 (the youngest was 32), their average age at marriage was almost at the end of their potential childbearing years.

As viewed in Table 2-C, almost ten percent of childless women died before their potential childbearing years were over. More than half of these (10) were under the age of thirty. The average age at marriage for all eighteen was 24.7, which was somewhat older than the average age at marriage for women in the entire database, but almost three years younger than the aggregate of childless females.

Table 2-C. Mortality of Married Database Childless Women During Their Years of Fecundity (15-45)

Age category	N	% of all childless women	Median age at marriage	Median length of marriage
under 45	18	9.2%	24.7	4.0 years
under 35	14	7.2%	24.5	2.5 years
under 30	10	5.1%	23.0	1.7 years

For that reason, age, in and of itself, is not an explanatory factor for the childlessness of these women. Before their deaths, they were married an average of four years, although those under thirty were married less than half that time. Unfortunately, causes of death for these women are not known. It is surmised that many were "sickly" at the time of their marriage, and therefore unlikely to have children. Others may have been carried off suddenly by disease (devastating outbreaks of such diseases as cholera and scarlet fever were not unknown in the 1800s). Still others may actually have become pregnant and died during a miscarriage or as a result of childbirth. As remarked in the previous research inquiry, nineteenth century rates of mortality for females aged fifteen to forty-five were markedly higher than that for males. Further, causes of death, especially with regard to stillborn children, or children dying during childbirth (or soon after), were often ignored in official records and genealogies because the event was so common (Peterson 1969:496-500).[2]

---

[2] See further comments on the effects of such under-enumeration in the previous and fourth research inquiries of this volume.

In a small percentage of instances, husbands died while their wives were in their childbearing years (Table 2-D). Of the 195 childless wives, eight (4.1%) of their husbands died while they were still of childbearing age.

Table 2-D. Database Husbands' Deaths During Childbearing Years	
Number of husband's deaths	8 (4.1% of childless women)
Wife's median age at marriage	26.5
Wife's median age at husband's death	32.5
Husband's median age at marriage	26.0
Husband's median age at death	33.0
Median length of marriage	4.5 years (4 were two years or less)

On average, these women married in their mid-twenties, and were in their early thirties when their husbands passed on. Their husbands tended to be about the same age as their wives at time of marriage. The median age of their deaths was thirty-three. The average length of these marriages was four and a half years, but four of the eight women were married two years or less. Given this information about age, it is suspected that the prime factor operating here was the health of the husband during these brief marriages. Presumably, their physical conditions were such as to preclude much thought of having children. It is interesting to note that, of these eight young widows, only one remarried. Her second marriage was at the age of forty-five, and she remained childless.

Nineteen (9.7%) of the childless women married widowers (see Table 2-E). Three of these widowers were without children, but were all over forty years of age at the time of their second marriages (forty, forty-eight, and fifty-three). However, sixteen widowers had children, thirteen with two or more. Further, thirteen of these widowers had at least one child under the age of twelve (eight had two or more). Half of the widowers remarried less than three years after the deaths of their first wives and, on average, were in their early to mid forties when they did so. Second wives (all of whom were marrying for the first time) had a median age of thirty-eight at the time of the wedding. Only five were younger than thirty.

Table 2-E. Database Childless Women Who Married Widowers	
Total marrying widowers	19 (9.7%)
Number marrying widowers with children	16 (8.2%), 13 with two or more children
Number marrying widowers with children < 12	13 (6.7%), 8 with two or more < 12
Widower remarriage median	3 years
Widower remarriage age median	43.5
Second wife marriage age median	38.0
Second wives under 30	5

It is clear than these widowers were seeking step-mothers for their children, rather than women who were expected to bear children of their own. Indeed, both widowers and their second wives began their marriages at ages which precluded much prospect of childbirth. This age consideration may, in fact, have played a major role in mate selection. That is, a middle-aged widower with children could very well have been seeking an older, more mature second mate who had recognized domestic proficiencies. For their part, these second wives, while marrying into "instant families," were trading the stigma of continued spinsterhood for the prestige of marriage, thus enhancing their standing in the community.

Summary and Conclusions

In the 1800s, a still heavily agrarian America valued childbirth. Nonetheless, there were a small but significant proportion of married females who remained childless. While much of this infertility, no doubt, had physical roots, the data here demonstrate that social factors (or at the very least, socio-medical factors) were also at play.

Roughly one out of every eight married females in the author's genealogical database was childless. A major reason for this was simply age. As a group, their median age at marriage was the late twenties, significantly later in life than was the norm at the time. While still hypothetically fecund, they were nonetheless in age groups which typically exhibit lowered fertility. Further, more than a fourth of these women were significantly younger than their husbands. That is, their spouses were often at an age when the husbands were less likely to sire, or, perhaps, even desire any children. Conversely, in a small number of cases, the wife was significantly *older* than her husband, and married at an age when the probability of childbirth was remote.

In roughly one out of nine instances, either the wife or the husband died an early death. In most of these instances, the marriage itself was quite short. While some of these wives may very well have died in childbirth, which went unrecorded, an equally likely explanation is that the spouse who died suffered from chronically poor health. This would engender a situation where both medical and family advice probably would encourage the couple to avoid pregnancy, which would arguably endanger an already precarious physical condition.

Finally, one in ten of the childless women was the second wife of the man she married. These women tended to marry when they were approaching middle age, and they tended to marry middle-aged widowers who had children from previous marriages. Rather than seeking wives for the purpose of starting, or, more accurately, expanding their families, these men were seeking women who would care for already existing households and the children in them. Further, it must be kept in mind that, for females, status and social position centered on the family. The only "occupation" to which the nineteenth century woman could aspire acceptably was wife and mother. Therefore, for an aging woman, movement from the much less respected status of spinster to the highly desired statuses of spouse and parent was a potent spur for marriage, even if into an already existing family.

It is very difficult, if not impossible, to gauge the proportion of nineteenth century women who were childless for reasons other than pure reproductive inability. Nonetheless, the data here demonstrate clearly that infertility in this era had social as well as physical bases. Indeed, if the desire for children was overwhelming in more of these childless families, adoption was a viable option. However, only one of this investigation's childless women exercised this alternative when, at the age of forty-three, she adopted one child. This is further support for the contention that, in spite of social pressures for having families, some nineteenth century couples preferred childlessness.

REFERENCES

Bell, Robert F. 1975. *Marriage and Family Interaction*. Homewood, IL: Dorsey Press.

Benokraitis, Nijole V. 2005. *Marriage and Families: Changes, Choices, and Constants* (Fifth Edition). Upper Saddle River, NJ: Pearson Prentice-Hall.

Duvall, Evelyn Millis. 1977. *Marriage and Family Development*. Philadelphia: J.B. Lippencott.

Kephart, William M. 1972. *The Family, Society, and the Individual*. Boston: Houghton Mifflin.

Leslie, Gerald R. and Elizabeth McLaughlin Leslie. 1977. *Marriage in a Changing World*. New York: John Wiley and Sons.

Peterson, William. 1969. *Population*. Second Edition. New York: MacMillan.

Saxton, Lloyd. 1972. *The Individual, Marriage, and the Family*. Belmont, CA: Wadsworth.

Smith, T. Lynn. 1960. *Fundamentals of Population Study*. Chicago: J.B. Lippencott.

Strong, Brian, Christine DeVault, and Theodore F. Cohen. 2005. *The Marriage and Family Experience* (Ninth Edition). Belmont, CA: Wadsworth.

Winch, Robert F. 1963. *The Modern Family* (Revised Edition). New York: Holt, Rinehart, and Winston.

RESEARCH INQUIRY 3:

ON NINETEENTH CENTURY
NEVER-MARRIEDS AND REMARRIEDS[1]

Introduction

Pressures to marry are intense. The view that adults not only *should* be married, but *must* be married is reinforced by unflattering stereotypes of the unmarried—a societal notion of the unmarried as social and personal failures, and a variety of social and economic sanctions against the unmarried (Bell 1975:156-158). Consequently, the proportion of unmarried adult males and females is quite low. Most sources state that only about five percent of adults remain single their entire lives (see Bell 1975:156; Duvall 1977:121; Leslie and Leslie 1977:4; Saxton 1972:191; T. T. Smith 1960:215; Williams, et. al. 2009:297).

The reasons for remaining unmarried are many and diverse (Bell 1975:158-167; Saxton 1972:196-197). For some, there is no "dating market." That is, there may be a sex ratio imbalance in an individual's own geographical, racial, ethnic, religious, educational, and/or age group. Some unmarrieds are socially inadequate, physically unattractive, or affected by debilitating physical or mental health conditions. Others place careers over marriage or have well-established, satisfying need fulfillment patterns they are reluctant to relinquish. Still others are heavily burdened

---

[1]   An earlier version of this study was presented at the 2009 annual meeting of the Georgia Sociological Association as "Never-Marrieds and Remarrieds in the Nineteenth Century."

with the care of ill or aging parents/relatives (which may include parental fixation). Certainly, hostility toward the opposite sex and homosexuality come into play.

Pressures to marry were just as intense, perhaps even more so, in the more agrarian American culture of the post-Colonial Seventeen and Eighteen Hundreds. Then, the family ideal was a husband and wife, together with several children, who formed a cohesive economic unit of agricultural production. In fact, this emphasis was so strong that, in early America, the then necessary expediency of common-law marriage quickly gained widespread acceptance (Bell 1975:248-249; Kephart 1972:140-141).

Nonetheless, in post-Colonial America, there was a certain incidence of bachelor—and spinsterhood. Because reliable statistics for this period of history are sketchy at best, rates are unknown. Indeed, the proportion of unmarried adults in the 1800s could have been higher than now. One observer (Saxton 1972:191) claims that, at the end of the nineteenth century, as many as twenty percent of adults never married. While this figure may be unrealistically high, it is nonetheless certain that there existed a noticeable proportion of the never-married. No doubt, many of today's reasons for not marrying were just as valid then. However, it is possible that certain family socioeconomic factors were at play. For instance, a very limited study of marriage patterns in colonial New England suggested that non-marriage might have been linked to economic dependence on parents, paternal primogeniture favoritism, and birth order (D. Smith 1978:91-96). Unwillingness of parents to give up control, questions of who inherited the family acres, and an obligation of younger children (especially females) to care for elderly parents may have been powerful reasons for nineteenth century adults to remain single.

There are not only pressures to marry, but to remarry after divorce or the death of a spouse. Remarriage rates in modern times, usually after divorce, are quite high and rather rapid. About eighty percent of the divorced are remarried within three years. Motivations include conformity to the expectation of marriage for all adults, sexual needs, and requirements for companionship and emotional support. The presence of children, especially young children, is also a strong motivation, in order to provide a "proper" family environment. (See Duvall 1977:62-63, 450; Kephart 1972:570-571; Leslie and Leslie 1977:341; Saxton 1972:269-270; Strong, et. al. 2005:513-515).

For remarriage after either divorce or death of a spouse, a number of characteristics have been noted (Bell 1975:559-565; Benokraitis 2005:459; Saxton 1972:268-269; Schwartz and Scott 2003:406-409; Winch 1963:340, 735-736). A higher proportion of men than women remarry, most likely because of age-specific sex ratios, and they remarry sooner. There is a greater age difference than in first marriages (about six years as opposed to about three years), but there is also a somewhat higher proportion (more than fifteen percent) of males *younger* than their wives in second marriages. Likelihood of remarriage, especially for women, is inversely related to age.

Much less is known about remarriage in the 1700 and 1800s. It is estimated that twenty to thirty percent of all marriages then were remarriages after the death of a spouse. This is a strong indication that remarriage was an expectation for both widows and widowers, especially those with young children (See Schwartz and Scott 2003:406). Widowers, particularly those with young children, tended to remarry sooner and more frequently than widows. However, there was a tendency for young and more elderly widows/widowers to remarry more quickly than those who were middle-age. Further, the older than man was, the greater was the age gap with his new wife, perhaps because of both age-specific sex ratios and the desire for a wife as a step-mother and/or mother of additional children. Conversely, the older the widow, the narrower the age gap with her new husband (perhaps pointing to the need for financial security and/ or dominance of companionship and emotional support as motivations for remarriage.

Never-Marrieds: Incidence and Traits

The study investigated marriageable males and females born prior to the year 1900. To be categorized as "marriageable," individuals in the target population had to have lived to at least the age of twenty and their age at death had to be known. Thus defined, a total of 2,192 marriageable males and 2,053 marriageable females were identified. Of these, eighty males (3.65 %) and fifty females (2.40 %) remained unmarried their entire lives.

This extraordinarily low non-marriage rate immediately obviates a number of associated factors, such as an imbalance in the sex ratio and the availability of potentially endogamous mates. However, others remain viable. While specific individual information on debilities, poor health, etc. is not available, some inferences can be made about the effect of physical condition by examining the age at death of the data pool's never-marrieds. As observed in Table 3-A, the median age at death for never-married males was about thirty and a half and that of never-married females a bit over thirty-four. Indeed, nearly seventy percent of never-married males[2] and fully sixty percent of never-married females died before they reached the age of forty. Presumably then, many, if not most, of these individuals did not marry because of serious health issues.

Age	Males		Females	
	N	%	N	%
21-29	39	48.8	20	40.0
30-39	16	20.0	10	20.0
40-49	8	10.0	2	4.0
50-59	9	11.2	6	12.0
60-69	4	5.0	3	6.0
70-79	4	5.0	3	6.0
80+	0	0.0	6	12.0
Total N	80	100.0	50	100.0
Median	30.4		34.2	

Table 3-A. Distribution of Database Never-Married Males and Females Born Prior to 1900, by Age at Death

---

[2] That the proportion of unmarried males is higher than that of females is attributable in part to war-related deaths and injuries. It is known that at least 6 males died in either the Civil War or World War I. Two more were seriously disabled in, and died as a result of, injuries sustained in the Civil War.

To examine the question of family economics (inheritance issues and care of elderly/infirm parents), family size and place in birth order of unmarrieds were scrutinized. As demonstrated in Table 3-B, both never-married males and never-married females came from large families, averaging seven children for males and somewhat better than seven children for females. While large families were not at all unusual in the 1800s, the families of never-marrieds were still larger than the average family size of the data pool as a whole (see Research Inquiry 1 and A. McCormick 1998; 2005). This gives some credence to the notion that, in the nineteenth century, the economics of a large family played a role in non-marriage.

The role of birth order, however, is less convincing. From Table 3-B, one sees that never-married males were at or toward the top of the birth order in their families. Seventeen of the twenty-five single males were one of the first four children born to their parents.

Table 3-B. Family Size and Birth Order Frequencies of Database Never-Married Males and Females, Age 40 and Older

	Males				Females				
No. of Children	Frequency	Birth Order	Family Freq.	Among Brothers Frequency	No. of Children	Frequency	Birth Order	Family Freq.	Among Sisters Frequency
1	0	1st	4	9	1	1	1st	5	10
2	1	2nd	4	7	2	0	2nd	6	6
3	0	3rd	4	4	3	3	3rd	4	2
4	2	4th	5	1	4	1	4th	2	2
5	3	5th	2	3	5	2	5th	1	
6	6	6th	0	0	6	2	6th	0	
7	2	7th	3	1	7	2	7th	0	
8	6	8th	2		8	3	8th	1	
9	3	9th	1		9	1	9th	0	
10	0	10th			10	1	10th	0	
11	0	11th			11	1	11th	0	
12	2	12th			12	1	12th	0	
13		13th			13	1	13th	1	
14					14	1			
N =	25		25	25	N =	20		20	20
Median	7.0		4.7	2.1	Median	7.5		1.3	1.5
Mean	7.0				Mean	7.2			

Further, twenty of these males were one of the first three males in the family. Indeed, more than a third were first-born sons. Finally, the data showed that the great majority of never-married males (N = 17) had other, often younger, adult brothers who did marry. As has been proposed, there may have been isolated instances of where a younger son failed to marry because of primogeniture or parental favoritism issues. However, the data here do not support this factor as a significant trend.

Likewise, birth order explanations do not support the non-marriage of the data pool's females. Table 3-B shows that never-married females tended to be born earlier among the family's children rather than later, as fifteen of the twenty were either the first, second, or third born among their siblings. Further, overwhelmingly, they were either the first or second born sister (only one was an only child). The data also show that these never-marrieds had other, usually younger, adult sisters (N = 13) who married. In the 1800s, there may very well have been pressures for older daughters to marry first (reference Laban's switch of Leah for Rachel as Jacob's first wife). There may also have been pressures for a daughter, especially a younger daughter, to devote her adult life caring for aged or infirm parents. However, the data do not support these explanations as an important reason not to marry.

Remarrieds: Incidence and Traits

Between 1750 and 1905, 1,014 males and 1,033 females in the data pool were married. Of these, seventy-four males (7.3%) and forty-one females (4.0%) remarried following the deaths of their first spouses. Because of the nature of family trees, affinal relatives are usually ignored after the death of consanguine kin.[3] Therefore, it is not unreasonable to guesstimate that at least 15% of data pool males and eight percent of data pool females eventually remarried after the deaths of their first mates. These figures are

---

[3] The author's great-grandmother, Emma Weaver McCormick Thresh, is an affinal relative in the Mansberger source. While her date of death is listed, her second marriage is not. However, in the Pershing source, where she is a consanguine relative, both her marriage to the author's great-grandfather and, following his death, her second marriage are listed.

not quite as high as estimates for the 1700 and 1800s, but still indicate the commonality of remarriage following the death of a spouse. Interestingly, six males and four females remarried after the deaths of their second spouses.

The analysis clearly supports previous findings that, prior to 1900, a higher proportion of males than females remarried. As seen in Table 3-C, there is also support for other contentions about remarriage in the 1700 and 1800s. For both remarried males and females, death of first spouses occurred between the ages of about twenty to the sixties and seventies, with median age in the mid-thirties for men and late twenties for women. Men tended to remarry a bit sooner, within an average of three years, in their late thirties, while women married within an average of about four years, in their early thirties. Although average age difference in data pool first marriages ranged between three to four years, widowers tended to be, on average, almost ten years older than their new wives.

Table 3-C. Characteristics of Database Remarrieds and Their New Families						
	Widowers			Widows		
	N	Range	Median	N	Range	Median
Age at 1st spouse's death	67	20 to 72	34.2	36	19 to 62	28.0
Age at remarriage	68	21 to 74	38.8	36	22 to 66	31.5
Years to remarriage	64	<1 to 21	3.0	34	<1 to 20	3.9
Age of 2nd spouse	55	17 to 66	25.8	35	24 to 81	36.0
Age difference (years)	56	-7 to 21	9.5	36	-30 to 11	-4.8
Younger/older than spouse	3 (4.1%)	-3 to -7	-3.5	7 (17.1%)	1 to 11	3.0
Number of 1st marriage children	74	0 to 13	2.4	41	0 to 6	1.6
Number of 1st marriage children <12	67	0 to 6	1.4	38	0 to 4	0.6
Number of children in remarriage	74	0 to 13	1.6	41	0 to 7	0.5

Widows were closer to the first-marriage age difference, averaging not quite five years younger than their second husbands. Interestingly, a small but significant proportion of widow remarriages involved males who were *younger*. Note that about seventeen percent of the widows married men younger than themselves, which virtually matches other findings. Finally, children seem to be an important factor in remarriage, especially for widowers, who had an average of two to three children in their first marriages. Widows had an average of one to two first-marriage children.

The presence of first-marriage children under the age of twelve also appears important. The final row of the table shows, clearly, having children born to the second marriage was much more important to widowers than it was to widows.

Further breakdown of these findings provides some specifics. Table 3-D examines the second spouse's age and age difference for remarrieds, by age at remarriage. First, inferentially, it is noted that age and likelihood of remarriage are related. For both males and females, very few over the age of fifty remarried. Indeed, for women, remarriage seems inversely related to age, as twenty-one (60%) of them were under the age of thirty-five when they re-wed. Second, it is observed that age differences vary markedly for both widowers and widows, based upon age at remarriage. For males, age gaps increased as the widower's age increased, narrowing again after the age of fifty.

Table 3-D. Database Second Spouse's Age and Age Difference, by Age at Remarriage

		Widowers			Widows	
Age at remarriage	N	Median age of 2nd spouse	Median age difference	N	Median age of 2nd spouse	Median age difference
20-29	5	23.0	2.5	15	30.0	-4.8
30-34	12	23.5	7.5	6	37.5	-8.0
35-39	15	26.0	10.0	4	37.5	0.0
40-49	19	32.0	13.8	5	40.0	1.0
50 and over	4	43.5	8.5	5	66.0	-8.0
Total	55	25.8	9.5	35	36.0	-4.8

This is perhaps related to a widower's desire to marry a wife capable of bearing children (or, just as likely, additional children). This would not be as important for men over fifty. Note, in fact, that median ages for second wives for all age groups, save for men over fifty, were in the twenties or early thirties. Widows, on the other hand, demonstrated a different pattern. Young widows tended to marry men four to eight years older than they were. Middle aged widows, however, tended to marry men virtually their own age. The age gap between more elderly widows and their new husbands increased, perhaps, at least in part, due to availability created by age-related sex ratios.

Rapidity of remarriage varied not only by gender, but by age. Table 3-E examines years to remarriage by age at remarriage. Except for those in their twenties (for whom the wait for remarriage was nearly identical), widowers tended to remarry more quickly than widows. While not hard and fast, there appears to be a mild association between rapidity of remarriage with age, with younger widows and widowers remarrying more quickly than the more elderly. Those over fifty waited by far the longest, with (contrary to what was indicated in the literature) widows marrying an average nine years after the deaths of their first husbands.

Table 3-E. Years to Remarriage, by Age at Remarriage, for Database Widowers and Widows				
	Widowers		Widows	
Age at remarriage	N	Median years to remarriage	N	Median years to remarriage
20-29	7	3.2	15	2.8
30-34	13	2.5	5	4.0
35-39	17	3.8	4	4.3
40-49	21	2.8	5	4.2
50 and over	6	4.5	5	9.0
Total	64	3.0	34	3.9

Much has been made of the relationship between remarriage and children. For widowers, several remarriage factors are examined in Table 3-F as they pertain to parental issues. Note first that widowers with no children and/or no children under the age of twelve, tended to be older than those with children (early forties), and they waited significantly longer to remarry (in the vicinity of five years). Further, while all widowers tended to marry young wives (on average, in their twenties) and the age gap tended to be rather large (on average, almost ten years), childless widowers and those with no children under age twelve tended to marry women older than widowers with children, especially those with children under twelve. It is also observed that there was a direct relationship between the number of children a widower had and the rapidity with which he remarried. Simply stated, the more children a widower had, the more quickly he acquired a second spouse. This was particularly true for widowers with children under the age of twelve.

Table 3-F. Database Widower Remarriage Factors by Number of First Marriage Children, Number of First Marriage Children under Age 12, and Number of Children in Remarriage

# of children	Number of First Marriage Children							
	Age at remarriage		Years to remarriage		Age of 2nd spouse		Age difference (years)	
	Median	N	Median	N	Median	N	Median	N
0	41.5	10	5.5	10	29.0	7	12.0	7
1	33.0	15	4.2	15	25.5	14	8.5	14
2	34.5	12	3.2	10	29.0	11	7.0	11
3	37.0	8	3.0	7	27.0	5	9.0	5
4	38.2	13	1.5	12	25.5	10	10.5	10
5 or more	44.5	10	1.5	10	32.5	8	13.0	9
Total	38.8	68	3.0	64	25.8	55	9.5	55
# of children	Number of First Marriage Children under Age 12							
	Age at remarriage		Years to remarriage		Age of 2nd spouse		Age difference (years)	
	Median	N	Median	N	Median	N	Median	N
0	42.5	20	4.5	18	29.5	16	13.0	16
1	34.5	16	4.2	15	25.0	13	8.0	13
2	34.3	9	2.0	9	25.0	6	2.5	6
3	42.0	11	2.0	11	27.5	10	13.0	10
4 or more	38.0	11	1.2	11	26.0	10	10.5	10
Total	38.8	67	3.0	64	25.8	56	9.5	55
# of children	Number of Children in Remarriage							
	Age at remarriage		Years to remarriage		Age of 2nd spouse		Age difference (years)	
	Median	N	Median	N	Median	N	Median	N
0	43.0	20	6.3	19	34.2	17	8.5	18
1	37.0	11	3.0	10	27.0	9	9.0	9
2	37.0	13	3.5	12	24.2	11	11.0	11
3	39.0	5	6.0	5	24.5	4	13.0	4
4	33.0	7	4.0	7	27.0	7	7.0	7
5 or more	36.0	12	3.0	11	25.0	7	9.0	7
Total	38.8	68	3.0	64	25.8	55	9.5	55

The desire for children, or more children, and its connection with remarriage is also evident from Table 3-F. Widowers whose second marriage produced no children tended to marry at a later age (early forties), waited longer (more than six years), and married somewhat older women (mid-thirties) than men who fathered children with their second wives. Further, the age difference between couples in childless second marriages tended to be narrower. On the other hand, continued parentage was apparently a strong remarriage motive for many widowers as about two-thirds had children by their second wives. Indeed, these wives tended to be in their mid-twenties, prime childbearing years. This was true for many older widowers as well, given the rather large age differences with their second wives.

For widows, examination of the relationship between remarriage and children shows both similarities and differences to the patterns shown by widowers. As viewed in Table 3-G, childless widows and widows with no young children, like their widower counterparts, tended to remarry when in their early forties and tended to wait longer (seven and a half years for childless widows; five years for widows with children under age twelve). Childless widows married much older second husbands (ten-year age gap), perhaps seeking security with more financially established middle-age males. However, widows with one or two children, especially those with children under the age of twelve, tended to marry second husbands more their own age. These would doubtless be younger men more willing to shoulder the responsibilities of raising young children (and possibly fathering still more). However, while for widowers there was a direct relationship between number of children, especially small children, and rapidity of remarriage, with widows the situation was reversed. The more children a widowed woman had in her first marriage, the longer it took her to find a second husband. This could be due to the unavailability of unmarried men created by differential age-sex ratios, coupled with the unwillingness of some males to marry into "instant" families.

Table 3-G. Database Widow Remarriage Factors by Number of First Marriage Children, Number of First Marriage Children under Age 12, and Number of Children in Remarriage

	Number of First Marriage Children							
# of children	Age at remarriage		Years to remarriage		Age of 2nd spouse		Age difference (years)	
	Median	N	Median	N	Median	N	Median	N
0	43.5	4	7.5	4	55.0	4	-10.0	5
1	29.0	13	2.5	12	31.0	12	- 1.0	12
2	33.0	11	3.2	10	34.0	11	- 5.0	11
3 or more	31.5	8	5.3	8	45.0	8	- 9.5	8
Total	31.5	36	3.9	34	36.0	35	- 4.8	36
	Number of First Marriage Children under Age 12							
# of children	Age at remarriage		Years to remarriage		Age of 2nd spouse		Age difference (years)	
	Median	N	Median	N	Median	N	Median	N
0	42.0	16	5.0	14	44.0	15	- 4.5	16
1	27.0	9	2.2	9	30.5	9	- 5.0	9
2	29.5	6	3.0	6	31.0	6	- 2.5	6
3 or more	28.0	5	4.0	5	40.0	5	-11.0	5
Total	31.5	36	3.9	34	36.0	35	- 4.8	36
	Number of Children in Remarriage							
# of children	Age at remarriage		Years to remarriage		Age of 2nd spouse		Age difference (years)	
	Median	N	Median	N	Median	N	Median	N
0	39.0	17	4.0	15	39.5	16	- 4.5	17
1	30.0	5	4.5	5	30.0	5	0.0	5
2	26.0	5	4.0	5	29.5	5	- 2.5	5
3 or more	29.0	9	2.5	9	36.0	9	- 7.0	9
Total	31.5	36	3.9	34	36.0	35	- 4.8	36

Nearly half of the remarrying widows had no further children, as opposed to less than a third of remarrying males. These tended to be women past or nearly past, the age of fecundity. Many, no doubt, had already bourn the children they wished to have. Fertility for the remainder was not high, especially when compared to the fertility of remarrying widowers. Because most had children in their first marriages, they were probably more in the market for husbands as step-fathers rather than husbands as procreators. Further, widows childless in their second marriages married men roughly equivalent in age (medians for both nearly forty). Widows bearing second-marriage children tended to be younger than their second husbands, but the age gap was not nearly as pronounced as that with widowers and their second wives. This accentuates fertility as a drive for remarriage among widowers.

Third Marriages

Given the mortality rates of the times, remarriages after the death of a second spouse were not unknown. While much rarer than first remarriages, they did occur. In the data pool, six men and four women married third spouses. The characteristics of these third marriages are presented in Table 3-H.

Table 3-H. Characteristics of Database Thrice-Marrieds and Their Third Families						
		Widowers			Widows	
	N	Range	Median	N	Range	Median
Age at 1st spouse's death	5	37 to 72	42.0	3	34 to 60	38.0
Age at remarriage	5	39 to 74	44.0	3	35 to 61[3]	45.0
Years to remarriage	5	1 to 7	2.0	3	1 to 7	1.5
Age of 3rd spouse	4	18 to 57[1]	35.0	3	35 to 70	52.0
Age difference (years)	4	3 to 26	13.5	3	-9 to 0	-7.0
Number of 1st marriage children	6	0 to 17	5.0	4	0 to 11	2.0
Number of 1st marriage children <12	6	0 to 5[2]	1.0	4	0 to 1[4]	0.2
Number of children in remarriage	6	0 to 8	1.0	4	0 to 2[5]	0.2

[1] Three of child-bearing age   [4] Only one had a child under 12
[2] Three had at least 2 children under 12   [5] Only one had children with third spouse
[3] One of child-bearing age

Unfortunately, given the paucity of numbers, only the sketchiest of conclusions may be drawn from this data. While the range of ages, for both widowers and widows, was sizeable, median ages at the death of the second spouse and that for remarriage were in the early stages of middle-age. These third marriages tended to come more quickly than second marriages, an average of about two years or so for both men and women. Widowers tended to marry much younger women and widows tended to marry rather older men.

For males, children tended to be a motivation for their third marriages. Four had children from their previous marriages, three of them with children under age twelve. Three widowers married women of childbearing age and had further children. Of the two remaining widowers, one had no children by any of his three wives. The other was in his seventies when remarrying for the third time and had seventeen children by his first two wives (who were all adults when he married his fifty-seven year old third spouse).

Children were much less of a factor for remarrying widows. While three of the four had children from their previous two marriages, only one had a child under age twelve (and just the one). Only one widow was of childbearing age upon her third marriage. She brought one child into the marriage (over age twelve) and bore two more with her third husband. Given that their third husbands were a bit more proximate to their own ages, as compared to the age gap between the widowers and their third spouses, these women were probably marrying more for reasons of companionship and, perhaps, economic security.

Discussion and Conclusions

The data pool findings on the never-married revealed some surprising results. First, the proportion of never-married adults was far lower than the literature indicated it might be. In modern times rates of non-marriage are in the vicinity of five percent. Some sources suggested that rates in the 1800s would be higher, perhaps significantly so. However, the non-marriage rates for the data pool were about three and a half percent and two and a half percent for males and females, respectively. This indicates that several demographic "non-availability" factors were simply not in play. Poor health, severe disabilities, and the like were probably very much in play, though, as evidenced by the fact that the majority of these never-married adults died before the age of forty.

While the socioeconomics of coming from a large family may have had an influence on non-marriage, birth order did not appear to be a significant element for either males or females. This does not preclude as factors either failure to inherit the farm or expectations to devote one's life to the care of elderly parents. Such conditions no doubt were a part of the culturally acceptable life situations for some individuals in the nineteenth century.[4]

Unfortunately, the nature of the data sources is such to preclude information on personality, career emphases, sexual orientation, psychological make-up, and the like. No doubt, such information would be critically useful in explaining the status of many never-marrieds in the data pool.[5]

Data pool findings on remarrieds tended to support expectations derived from the literature. While the data indicated an incidence of remarriage rather below estimates of what occurred in the 1700 and 1800s, it certainly was not at all uncommon. Further, findings bear out the view that widowers remarried more frequently and sooner than widows. Additionally, widowers tended to marry second wives much younger than themselves, wives usually in the childbearing years. Widows, on the other hand, tended to marry second husbands closer to their own age. However, the age gap between widows and their second husbands tended to be a bit greater than that with their first husbands. Not unsurprisingly, about one out of six widows married second husbands *younger* than they were. That proportionately fewer widows remarried, and that many of them who did married men younger than they, probably points to a narrower field of eligibles than that enjoyed by widowers (created, no doubt, by differential age-sex ratios).

Age was definitely related to probabilities of remarriage and its rapidity. Few males and females over the age of fifty entered into second marriages and they waited the longest of any age group. Most remarrying widowers were between the ages of thirty and fifty, and men in this age range tended to marry much younger women. Further, few of the remarrying widowers

---

[4] This can be supported with anecdotal evidence from the data pool. The author's great-great grandfather, Dr. James Irwin McCormick, died in 1881, leaving a widow (his second wife). She lived the remainder of her life with one of her daughters, who never married.

[5] The author had a set of distant brother-sister cousins who never married. Of the five siblings who lived well into adulthood, three (perhaps four—the records are unclear) never married. This is an unusually high number of unmarried adults in a single family, especially a farm family. One wonders what collectively led them to forgo, perhaps forsake, marriage.

were under the age of 30. Remarrying widows, on the other hand, were disproportionately young, remarried rather quickly, and tended to marry significantly older second husbands. Only widows approaching or at the end of fecundity married second husbands their own age, and they waited relatively long periods to do so. Inferentially, these findings indicate that childbearing capability was an important factor in nineteenth mate selection: Widowers desiring children (or more children) and widows hoping to attract a second mate.

Children were clearly an important factor motivating second (and for men, third) marriages. Both widowers and widows with no children from previous marriages, or no children under age twelve, remarried later in life and after longer periods of time. There was a direct relationship between number of children and rapidity of remarriage. Widowers with several children, especially under the age of twelve, remarried the most rapidly of all. Further, a preponderance of widowers married much-younger wives with a view toward having children and/or having more children.

With widows, however, there was an inverse relationship between number of children from the previous marriage and rapidity of remarriage. Young widows with a child or two remarried more frequently, more quickly, and were more likely to have further children in the second marriage. This, and that their second husbands were likely to be fairly close to them in age, suggests that continued fertility was an expectation in the remarriage. Older widows with more and older children married less frequently and less rapidly. Given age-sex differentials, this is not surprising, as the pool of eligible males dwindles with increasing age. Further, as pointed out above, older men preferred marrying much younger wives, who would prove to be more fertile. Indeed, fertility among remarried widows was remarkably low. More than half had no children, or no further children, at all. Only one-fourth had three or more children with their second husbands and these women tended to be in their twenties upon remarriage.

The few third marriages occurring within the data pool support this study's general findings. Widowers married third spouses who could care for children from the previous marriages and/or have further children. One elderly widower married a woman who was in her late fifties, presumably for companionship and care in his old age. Widows remarrying for a third time were close to the end or past childbearing age, did not have children under age twelve, and wed men reasonably close to their own ages. Therefore, these widows were probably remarrying for reasons of companionship and economic security.

Mate selection prior to the year 1900 was different than today being motivated by the more agrarian-oriented culture of the times. This study shows that marriage was a paramount expectation for all adults. Non-marriage rates were very low, and those who did not marry presumably were unmarriageable because of chronic poor health, as evidenced by their low life expectancies. Remarriage patterns strongly infer the importance of several mate selection factors. For young and middle-aged widowers, the care of young motherless children and the desire for more children were important considerations. For widows, keeping in mind that women then rarely worked outside the home, economic support for their children and themselves had to be considered.[6] For older widows and widowers, companionship and care in the later years of life were significant.

---

[6] The author's great-grandfather, William Henry Harrison McCormick, died in 1910 at the age of forty-seven. His widow Emma, my great-grandmother (mentioned above in footnote #2) remarried in 1916. In the author's possession are several letters she wrote to my grandfather, himself a relatively newly married man, during her six-year period of widowhood. Many of these letters contain expressions of gratitude for small amounts of money he had sent to her. His supplements to her income ceased upon her remarriage.

REFERENCES

Bell, Robert F. 1975. *Marriage and Family Interaction*. Homewood, IL: Dorsey Press.

Benokraitis, Nijole V. 2005. *Marriages and Families* (Fifth Edition). Upper Saddle River, NJ: Prentice-Hall.

Duvall, Evelyn Millis. 1977. *Marriage and Family Development* (Fifth Edition). Philadelphia: J.B. Lippencott.

Kephart, William M. 1972. *The Family, Society, and the Individual*. Boston: Houghton Mifflin.

Leslie, Gerald R. and Elizabeth McLaughlin Leslie. 1977. *Marriage in a Changing World*. New York: John Wiley and Sons.

McCormick, Albert E. 1998. "American Demographic Trends in the Nineteenth and Early Twentieth Centuries: A Genealogical Exploration." Pp. 28-44 in Albert E. McCormick, Jr. (ed.), *American Society: Readings in Social Behavior* (Third Edition). Needham Heights, MA: Simon and Shuster.

—.2005. "Using Genealogies to Examine Historical Social Structures." Presented at the annual meeting of the Georgia Sociological Association (October 22). St. Simon's Island, Georgia.

Saxton, Lloyd. 1972. *The Individual, Marriage, and the Family* (Second Edition). Belmont, CA: Wadsworth.

Schwartz, Mary Ann and Barbara Marliene Scott. 2003. *Marriages and Families: Diversity And Change* (Fourth Edition). Upper Saddle River, NJ: Prentice-Hall.

Smith, Daniel Scott. 1978. "Parental Power and Marriage Patterns: An Analysis of Historical Trends in Hingham, Massachusetts." Pp. 87-100 in Michael Gordon (ed.), *The American Family in Socio-Historical Perspective* (Second Edition). New York: St. Martin's Press.

Smith, T. Lynn. 1960. *Fundamentals of Population Study*. Chicago: J.B. Lippencott.

Strong, Brian, Christine DeVault, and Theodore F. Cohen. 2005. *The Marriage and Family Experience*. Belmont, CA: Thomson-Wadsworth.

Williams, Brian K., Stacey C. Sawyer, and Carl M. Wahlstrom. 2009. *Marriage, Family, and Intimate Relationships* (Second Edition). Boston: Pearson.

Winch, Robert F. 1963. *The Modern Family* (Revised Edition). New York: Holt, Rinehart, and Winston.

RESEARCH INQUIRY 4:

ON NINETEENTH CENTURY
INFANT MORTALITY AND CHILD-NAMING[1]

Introduction

Naming ceremonies, baptisms, and similar social presentation rituals are usually the first rites of passage through which individuals pass. This is because birth itself is not necessarily adequate for acceptance into the group. Rather, a formal presentation rite represents the *process* of becoming a member of society (Vivelo 1978). Until then, as with any rite of passage's transitional phase, an infant is in social limbo, occupying a social position of anonymity and an absence of status (Kottak 1996).

In a representative sample of the world's cultures, Barry and Paxson (1971) found that only eleven percent had no presentation rituals. About forty percent held such ceremonies within two months of birth, while nearly half waited until the child was older, held two or more ceremonies, and/or showed marked concern with such rites. In many cultures, infant mortality is so high that presentation or naming ceremonies are postponed until it seems likely that the child will survive. Until that time, the child does not have a social identity. If it dies, its death is faced with stoicism and equanimity. Likely, the dead child is not publicly mourned, nor are

---

[1] An earlier version of this study was presented at the 2004 annual meeting of the Georgia Sociological Association and published in *The Journal of Public and Professional Sociology*, Vol. 3, Iss. 2 (2010) as "Infant Mortality and Child-Naming: An Exploration of American Trends."

funeral rites held for it (Beals 1980; Richards 1972; Scheper-Hughes 1989).

In contemporary U.S. society, rates of infant mortality are relatively low. Historically, however, this has not always been the case. In colonial America, ten to thirty percent of children did not survive the first year of life. There was a high probability that a typical family would suffer the loss of at least one infant (Vinovskis 1978:553-554). In analyses of genealogical information, A. McCormick (1998; 2005—see also Research Inquiry 1 in this volume) showed that infant mortality rates reached their currently low levels only well into the twentieth century.[2]

Research Inquiry 1 also indicated rather high nineteenth century infant mortality rates, but not nearly as high as expected. Much of the discrepancy was explained by the occurrence of *under-enumeration*, a problem biasing socio-historical statistics. Chronicles, reports, and records often reflected *effective* rather than actual fertility because the true number of a woman's births was not necessarily recorded. Not infrequently, infants dying soon after birth were matter-of-factly ignored (See Peterson 1969:496-500 for elaboration on factors affecting historical fertility data).[3]

When updating and examining his genealogical files, the author noticed a fairly large number of instances in which deceased children went unnamed. Instead, they were identified simply as "infant," or sometimes

---

[2]   The author's genealogical data indicate that it was not at all unusual for a couple to lose at least one child. Often, a couple would lose more, sometimes many more. For example, a fourth great-uncle of the author had twelve children, only four of whom survived to their teen-age years. Four died before the age of one, two more before the age of five, and another by the age of nine. One of the author's third great-grandparents, Isaac and Frances Truxal Pershing, had fourteen children, of whom eight died in infancy or early childhood.

[3]   The problem of under-enumeration is illustrated anecdotally by one of the data sources for the author's great-great-grandmother, Rachael Black McCormick. She died at the age of thirty-five while giving birth to twins, who also died. The source in question reported only the births of her five living children. Pertinent to the thrust of this study, two other sources authenticated the twins' births, but indicated that the infants were not named.

as "baby" or "child." Sometimes gender was indicated, sometimes not. Sometimes the additional information "unnamed" was added. As leaving a deceased child unnamed is a rare event these days, the link between this phenomenon and past rates of infant mortality, coupled with under-enumeration, could not be merely coincidental. The present study seeks further insights into the historically not uncommon custom of allowing dead infants to go unnamed. The results shed light on once prevalent attitudes toward both death and notions as to when, socially, life began.

Unnamed Infants: Incidence

The data yielded sixty-nine instances of deceased unnamed infants from the year 1800 to the year 1979. These are shown, by decade, in the third column of Table 4-A. These are compared to the total number of infant deaths (defined as children who died before reaching the age of one), by decade, for the same time period.

Table 4-A. Total Number of Database Infant Deaths versus Number Unnamed, 1800-1979.

Year	Infant Deaths	Infants Unnamed	% Unnamed	No Gender
1800-1819	3	1	33.3%	0 (---------)
1820-1829	4	2	50.0%	2 (100.0%)
1830-1839	9	1	11.1%	0 (---------)
1840-1849	13	4	30.8%	1 (25.0%)
1850-1859	24	6	25.0%	2 (33.3%)
1860-1869	26	11	42.3%	10 (90.0%)
1870-1879	41	4	9.8%	2 (50.0%)
1880-1889	35	8	22.3%	5 (62.5%)
1890-1899	54	5	9.3%	2 (40.0%)
1900-1909	58	13	22.4%	5 (38.5%)
1920-1919	59	7	11.9%	3 (42.9%)
1920-1929	29	4	13.8%	0 (---------)
1930-1939	5	0	0.0%	0 (---------)
1940-1949	4	1	25.0%	0 (---------)
1950-1959	3	1	33.0%	1 (100.0%)
1960-1969	7	0	0.0%	0 (---------)
1970-1979	3	1	33.3%	1 (100.0%)
Total	377	69	18.3%	34 (49.3%)

The table reveals that the *number* of infant deaths and unnamed infants peaked around the turn of the nineteenth century. It is also interesting to note that the proportion of unnamed infants to total infant deaths is often high and averages nearly twenty percent overall. Further, about half of the unnamed infants did not even have their genders indicated in the family records. Their existences were merely noted as "deceased infant." This was especially prevalent in about an eighty-year period beginning in the mid-1800s. Note that ten out of eleven unnamed infants in the 1860s did not have their genders indicated.

Pure numbers, however, tell only part of the story. More is revealed when *rates* of infant mortality and unnamed infants (i.e., infant deaths and unnamed infants per 1,000 born in the same time period) are examined. These are depicted in Figure 4-A.

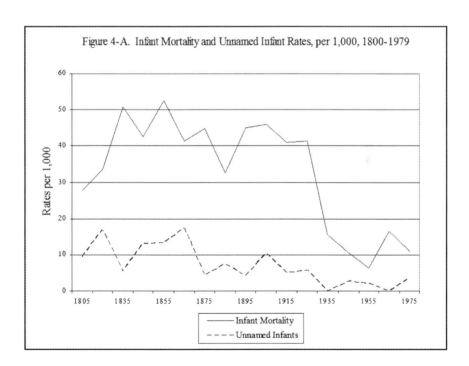

Figure 4-A. Infant Mortality and Unnamed Infant Rates, per 1,000, 1800-1979

Generally, rates of infant mortality were high in the 1800s and early 1900s, dropping rapidly in the 1930s. Rates of unnamed infants tended to follow this pattern, giving support to the notion that allowing deceased infants to remain unnamed is strongly related to higher levels of infant mortality. It is interesting to observe that the rate of not naming a child peaked in the 1860s at a time when the overall infant mortality rate declined a bit. Speculatively (and reinforced by the observation above on gender identification) this could be a side effect of a time when the nation was in great turmoil, a time when even less attention could be given to an infant who had died prematurely.

More is learned when age at death is examined. Precise birth and death dates were available for 230 out of the 308 deceased named infants and thirty-five out of the sixty-nine deceased unnamed infants. It is observed in Table 4-B that close to three-fourths of the named infants had precise dates of birth and death recorded, while this was true for only half of the unnamed infants. The more striking finding, though, is that unnamed infants usually lived only a very short time after birth.

Table 4-B. Database Infant Longevity: Named versus Unnamed		
Died (Non-cumulative):	Named Infants	Unnamed Infants
Day of birth	28 (12.2%)	23 (65.7%)
Within 1 week	22 (9.6%)	5 (14.3%)
Within 1 month	22 (9.6%)	5 (14.3%)
Within 2 months	22 (9.6%)	1 (2.9%)
Within 3 months	11 (4.8%)	1 (2.9%)
Within 4 months	19 (8.3%)	------------
Within 5 months	18 (7.8%)	------------
Within 6 months	18 (7.8%)	------------
Within 7 months	9 (3.9%)	------------
Within 8 months	11 (4.8%)	------------
Within 9 months	11 (4.8%)	------------
Within 10 months	15 (6.5%)	------------
Within 11 months	11 (4.8%)	------------
Within 12 months	13 (5.7%)	------------

Total	230	35
Mean Days of Life	126.2	6.1
Median Days of Life	114	0
Precise Birth and Death Dates	230 out of 308 (74.7%)	35 out of 69 (50.7%)

About two-thirds died on the days of their births. Only two lived more than a month. Named infants, however, lived an average of roughly four months. Only about one in ten died on the days of their births and nearly forty percent lived more than six months.

Summary and Conclusions

Literature on rites of passage indicates that newborns do not become "persons" until they exhibit likelihood to survive. It is then that the child undergoes some sort of presentation ceremony and is introduced to the community. Until that time, the child does not have a social identity. For a child, this period of status limbo is directly linked to rates of infant mortality. In the United States, rates of infant mortality were quite high until well after onset of the 1900s. It would then be expected that baptisms and naming ceremonies were more than the perfunctory rituals they are now.

Extensive genealogical information available to the author, for the years 1800 to 1979, supports this contention. In this time period, of 377 infants who died before the age of one year, sixty-nine were unnamed. That is, nearly one out of five infant deaths traced in the study did not go through a baptism or naming ceremony. Further, half of the deceased unnamed infants did not even have their genders recorded. The data also demonstrate a strong link between high rates of infant mortality and allowing deceased infants to remain unnamed. This was notably the case for infants who died shortly after birth, especially if death occurred on the day of birth. Conversely, the longer a child lived, the more likely it was to have been given a name.

The findings suggest that the question, "When does life begin?" has a social/ anthropological as well as a biological or religious answer. In the cultural history of American society, it is clear from these findings that birth itself was not a guarantee of full-fledged admission into social life. Rather, in the face of high rates of infant mortality, a newborn was more of an "it" until it could prove itself capable of some viability. In other words, the cost of investing, especially emotionally investing, in a newborn was too high if the child was likely to die. By considering a newborn as something less than human, grief at the death of a child (which can easily become psychologically and socially debilitating, both in the short term and the long term) is minimized.[4] In societies with high rates of infant mortality, the living must arrive at coping mechanisms signifying that life goes on. One way of achieving this is by delaying naming and presentation ceremonies until the survival of a child is more likely.

---

[4] In 1946, a close relative of the author lost a (named) child, who died two days after birth. For more than sixty years, this relative went into a (fortunately) temporary bout of severe depression on the anniversary days of the child's very brief life.

REFERENCES

Barry, Herbert III and Leonora M. Paxson. 1971. "Infancy and Early Childhood: Cross-Cultural Codes 2." *Ethnology* 10:466-508.

Beals, Alan R. 1980. *Gopalpur: A South Indian Village.* New York: Holt, Rinehart, and Winston.

Kottak, Conrad Phillip. 1996. *Mirror for Humanity.* New York: McGraw-Hill.

McCormick, Albert E., Jr. 1998. "American Demographic Trends in the Nineteenth and Early Twentieth Centuries: A Genealogical Exploration." Pp. 28-44 in *American Society: Readings In Social Behavior*, edited by Albert E. McCormick, Jr. Needham Heights, MA: Simon and Schuster Custom Publishing.

—.2005. "Using Genealogies to Examine Historical Social Structures." Presented at the annual meeting of the Georgia Sociological Association (October 22). St. Simons Island, Georgia.

Peterson, William. 1969. *Population.* Second Edition. New York: MacMillan.

Richards, Cara E. 1972. *People in Perspective.* Second Edition. New York: Random House.

Scheper-Hughes, Nancy. 1989. "Death without Weeping." *Natural History* October:8-16.

Vinovskis, Maris A. 1978. "Angel's Heads and Weeping Willows: Death in Early America." Pp. 546-563 in *The American Family in Social-Historical Perspective*, edited by Michael Gordon. New York: St. Martin's Press.

Vivelo, Frank Robert. 1978. *Cultural Anthropology Handbook*. New York: McGraw-Hill.

RESEARCH INQUIRY 5:

ON NINETEENTH CENTURY OCCUPATIONAL AND STRUCTURAL MOBILITY: FROM THE OLD TO THE NEW MIDDLE CLASS[1]

Introduction

Analytical interest in social class was given impetus by Marx's postulations of discrete class-conscious strata based upon their relationship to the economy. Weber, however, later put forward that class position was based upon a not necessarily consistent combination of wealth and income, status and prestige, and power. In Weber's view, because of the resulting varied combinations of these factors, social strata were not well-defined, polarized groups, but collectivities that may or may not develop a sense of commonality (Broom and Selznick 1968:154; *Encyclopedia of Sociology* 1974:44-6; Martindale 1960:446-50). Following Weber, most current perspectives see class stratification systems as highly complex, posing very difficult problems of conceptualization and analysis (Mayer and Buckley 1970:15). As a result, there is no broad consensus about how modern class structure should be characterized (Sanderson 1999:199). Attempts to delineate class structure, such as those by Warner and Rossides, have not been definitive, but rather have pointed out the ambiguities and anomalies in strata demarcations (Broom and Selznick 1968:165; Rossides

---

[1]   An earlier version of this study was presented at the 2010 annual meeting of the Georgia Sociological Association as "From the Old to the New: A Genealogical Look at Middle Class Occupational and Structural Mobility."

1990; Sanderson 1999:199-204). Most observers, therefore, conclude that American class structure is fluid, flexible, and ever-changing (Mayer and Buckley 1970:16-7, 137).

Several factors contribute to the complexities of stratification. A driving force has been, and continues to be, massive technological development. Society's rapid transformation from an agrarian through an industrial to a post-industrial economy extensively continues to expand and diversify society's division of labor. Technological advances have come with a concomitant knowledge explosion and a rise of large-scale bureaucracies. All of this has resulted in a proliferation of new, more specialized, and continually mutating occupations. Further, American society has been characterized by an important amount of social mobility, which has acted to enhance class fluidity and the blurring of class distinctions (Mayer and Buckley 1970:4-7, 144-5; Ritzer 1977:8-12; Sanderson 1999:205).

Nowhere are the complexities of social class more evident than with the middle class. The largest and most amorphous of American social strata, it is a level comprised, broadly speaking, of persons with similar amounts of wealth and prosperity. However, it is not a single, homogeneous mass, but rather a very large and diversified series of segments, with different and often contradictory interests (Martindale 1960:646; Mills 1951:351-2). It is basically white-collar, and its upper reaches are comprised of professionals and upper management. It ranges down through farm and business small entrepreneurs, semiprofessionals, and lower managers to clerical workers and retail sales personnel. Some students of social class, however, place foremen, craftsmen, tradesmen, and similar blue collar workers in the middle class as well, based upon income and life style factors (Henslin 2007:268-9; Mills 1951).

The middle class has been marked with significant social mobility. Historically speaking, a great deal of this mobility has been structural, due to the effects of the Industrial and Post-Industrial Revolutions. However, numerous contemporary studies indicate that this mobility has been limited. These studies tend to show that a majority of sons enter occupations different from their fathers, but this mobility tends to be more horizontal than vertical. When vertical mobility occurs, it tends to be to one level up or down (Duberman 1976:105-8; Mayer and Buckley 1970:139-41).

Unfortunately, there is very little data on social mobility prior to 1900 (Duberman 1976:105). Perhaps the most widely known analysis is that by Mills in his seminal work *White Collar* (1951). As late as 1870, America was primarily agrarian. In that era, what Mills terms the "old" middle class was comprised principally of free small entrepreneurs—farmers, merchants, cottage manufacturers, professionals—who owned their sources of livelihood. The technological revolutions brought about a "new" middle class—managers, staff professionals, salespeople, office workers—who, through salaries, were dependent upon the property of others for a livelihood. By 1940, the old middle class had suffered significant decline, particularly among free farmers. Concomitantly, the new middle class has grown by leaps and bounds (Martindale 1960:462-3; Mayer and Buckley 1970:144-5; Mills 1951; Ritzer 1977:13-21).

It must be remarked that virtually all work in stratification has focused on the wealth, income, occupations, prestige, and power of men. Traditionally, the role of women was familial and home-centered and they derived their social standing, depending upon marital status, from their fathers or their husbands. Occupational participation had to be subordinate to childbearing and child-rearing. If a woman was in the "outside" work force, it was before and/or after child-rearing, was intermittent or part-time, or was a full-time career without marriage or without children. Further, "suitable" female occupations were sex-labeled and included only those "helping" positions thought to require "feminine" traits, such as nurse, teacher, librarian, social worker, sales worker, or clerical staff. These "women's" occupations were usually low skilled and low-paid (Duberman 1976:110-2, 282-9; *Encyclopedia of Sociology* 1974:260; Ritzer 1977:330, 355).

The purpose of the current inquiry is to take a closer look at the historic transition from an old to a new middle class society through the examination of genealogical records. This is particularly important because very few empirical stratification inquiries have reached back prior to 1900. This investigation will examine the occupations pursued by six generations of related families, beginning with those born in the early 1700s and ending with those born in the late 1800s and early 1900s. Focus will be centered on the occupational shifts that occurred with the decline of the old middle class and the rise of the new. Further, this inquiry will explore some idiosyncrasies of the old middle class, such as the rather common phenomenon of simultaneously pursued secondary occupations and the utilization of certain occupations as stepping stones to others. Finally, a look will be taken at the occupational status position of women in this era, as measured both by marriage and by their entrance into the work force.

Data and Method

The usual practice in gauging social mobility is to examine changes in inter- and intragenerational occupational prestige. Therefore, this investigation traced occupations, where known, for males and females beginning with the first generation of the database (individuals born in the early 1700s) through five subsequent generations, concluding with individuals born in the late 1800s and early 1900s. In all, the occupations of 401 individuals were identified, 355 of them male and forty-six female. The occupations are distributed generationally as depicted in Table 5-A.

Table 5-A. Distribution of Identified Database Occupations, by Generation

Generation	Approx. Birth Year Range	Male N	Female N	Total N
1	1710-1725	3	0	3
2	1740-1780	11	2	13
3	1785-1820	32	1	33
4	1820-1860	96	1	97
5	1850-1890	99	11	110
6	1880-1920	114	31	145
Total		355	46	401

To facilitate generational comparisons, these livelihoods were then sorted into broad occupational categories, as suggested by the literature on the old and new middle classes and by contemporary occupational paradigms. These categories, the occupations that comprise them, and brief parenthetical categorization criteria are found in Appendix G.

While a unique source of sociological information, a genealogical database is not without its limitations, as have been described earlier in this volume's Prologue. Specific to this investigation, there are several qualifications. First, the very nature of a genealogy makes generalizations difficult, because (as observed in Table 5-A) there are very few people in the early generations—the "family tree" effect. Second, in agrarian times, fertility was high and extended over much a woman's period of fecundity. Thus, it was not at all unusual for the last of a large brood of children to be contemporary with nephews and nieces born to the now married first of the brood. This blurs and confuses the temporal meaning of "generation," as observed in the rather interesting generational birth year ranges found in Table 5-A.[2] Third, genealogical data is very frequently incomplete. In this instance, it is estimated that the 401 individuals about whom occupations are known encompass about fifteen to twenty percent of the total number of adults comprising the first six generations of the database.

In addition, while the use of occupations to measure mobility has a strong place, it is not without its pitfalls. Occupations are not necessarily consistent with other stratum factors, such as income or educational attainment. Further, social views on and evaluations of particular occupations can, and do, fluctuate over time (see Broom and Selznick 1968:167-8; Duberman 1976:22-41). Nonetheless, this investigation's findings further advance appreciation of the American middle class's socio-historic evolution.

---

[2] For example, the one of the author's third great-grandmothers, Jane Mansberger Black, was married at the age of 15, had her first child at the age of 16, and her last of 15 children at the age of 43. Her oldest child (a daughter) had four children before her mother bore her last child. In fact, the mother bore four more children *after* her oldest daughter had her first child. Therefore, a number of these aunt/uncles and nephew/nieces were, in fact, cotemporaries.

Findings:
Intergenerational Structural Mobility

Table 5-B reveals that, occupationally, the first three generations of the male database were rooted firmly in the old middle class. As would be expected in an agrarian society, nearly three-fourths were farm proprietors.

Table 5-B. Generational Distribution of Database Male Occupations, by Old Middle, New Middle, and Blue Collar Class Categories

Occupational Category	Generational Number					Total
	1 and 2	3	4	5	6	
Professional	2 (14.3%)	1 (3.1%)	12 (12.5%)	14 (14.1%)	13 (11.4%)	42 (11.8%)
Proprietor, Farm	12 (85.7%)	23 (71.9%)	49 (51.0%)	30 (30.3%)	13 (11.4%)	127 (35.8%)
Proprietor, Business	------	4 (12.5%)	13 (13.5%)	14 (14.1%)	9 (7.9%)	40 (11.3%)
Proprietor, Skilled Trade	------	2 (6.3%)	9 (9.4%)	2 (2.0%)	6 (5.3%)	19 (5.4%)
Total Old Middle:	14 (100.0%)	30 (93.8%)	83 (86.5%)	60 (60.5%)	41 (36.0%)	228 (64.3%)
Executive Management	-----	------	7 (7.3%)	18 (18.2%)	13 (11.4%)	38 (10.7%)
Semi-professional	------	------	4 (4.2%)	5 (5.1%)	21 (18.4%)	30 (8.4%)
Supervisor Management	------	------	1 (1.0%)	5 (5.1%)	18 (15.8%)	24 (6.8%)
White-Collar	------	------	1 (1.0%)	2 (2.0%)	5 (4.4%)	8 (2.3%)
Office Personnel/Staff	------	-----	------	4 (4.0%)	3 (2.6%)	7 (2.0%)
Total New Middle:	-----	-----	13 (13.5%)	34 (34.3%)	60 (52.6%)	107 (30.1%)
Skilled Trade	------	1 (3.1%)	------	2 (2.0%)	9 (7.9%)	12 (3.4%)
Laborer	------	1 (3.1%)	------	3 (3.0%)	4 (3.5%)	8 (2.3%)
Total Blue Collar:	------	2 (6.3%)	------	5 (5.1%)	13 (11.4%)	20 (5.6%)
Total All Occupations	14 (100.0%)	32 (100.0%)	96 (100.0%)	99 (100.0%)	114 (100.0%)	355 (100.0%)

The rest were professionals (physicians or ministers) or proprietors of businesses or skilled trades. Of the two blue collar occupations in the third generation, one was a canal company employee and the other, the laborer, was a stage driver. Note that the third generation, born roughly in the late 1700 and early 1800s, would have begun their occupational careers toward the beginning of the Industrial Revolution. Indeed, these two wages earners, as employees of then nascent, but increasingly important, transportation industries perhaps were occupational harbingers of impending change.

It is with the fourth generation, who would have begun working, for the most part, in the mid-1800s, that new middle class positions began to appear. Although seven out of eight in this generation still followed old middle class pursuits, the proportion of farm proprietors had fallen to about half. The fifth and sixth generations' occupational distributions demonstrate just how rapidly precipitous the decline in the old middle class was. By the sixth generation, when occupations were first entered in the early 1900s, only about one in three relied on earnings from their own property, while almost two-thirds, while in mostly middle-class positions, worked for others.

It is clear from the data that these losses in old middle class membership came almost entirely from the ranks of farm proprietors. While farming was the dominant occupation among those in the first three generations, about one in ten among the sixth generation farmed. Note, on the other hand, that the proportions of self-employed professionals and proprietors of business and skilled trades remained roughly steady throughout all six generations.

As a side observation, the findings conform to contemporary notions concerning intergenerational mobility. The mobility from old to new middle class tended to be horizontal. Most of the children of old middle class parents who entered the new middle class did so through managerial, semi-professional, supervisory, or white-collar positions. When vertical mobility occurred, it tended to be one step up or one step down. Very few entered into blue collar pursuits and even here (as pointed out above) some observers classify many in the skilled trades as middle class on the basis of income and life style.

Findings:
The Old Middle Class and Simultaneous Pursuits

Unlike the contemporary age of increasing occupational complexity and specialization, it was not at all unusual in the old middle class for individuals to follow multiple occupational pursuits *simultaneously*. Eighty individuals in the database, or about twenty percent, followed at least one other pursuit concurrent with their primary occupation. Indeed, the average was 1.6 secondary occupations. As observed in Table 5-C, simultaneous employments were not at all unusual before the Industrial Revolution took effect, as evidenced by the proportion so engaged in the first three generations of the database. Beginning with the fourth generation though (in the mid to latter part of the 1800s), the proportion of those engaged in simultaneous pursuits declined rapidly. This would not be unexpected, as industrialization and increasing specialization were beginning to take hold at this time.

Table 5-C. Generational Distribution of Database Simultaneous Occupational Pursuits, by Old Middle, New Middle, and Blue Collar Class Categories

Occupational Category	Generational Number					
	1 and 2	3	4	5	6	Total
Professional	-----	-----	3 (11.1%)	4 (20.0%)	2 (20.0%)	9 (11.3%)
Proprietor, Farm	7 (100.0%)	14 (87.5%)	18 (66.7%)	10 (50.0%)	3 (30.0%)	52 (65.0%)
Proprietor, Business	-----	2 (12.5%)	3 (11.1%)	2 (10.0%)	-----	7 (8.8%)
Proprietor, Skilled Trade	-----	-----	1 (3.7%)	-----	-----	1 (1.3%)
Total Old Middle:	7 (100.0%)	16 (100.0%)	25 (92.6%)	16 (80.0%)	5 (50.0%)	69 (86.3%)
Executive Management	-----	-----	1 (3.7%)	2 (10.0%)	-----	3 (3.8%)
Semi-professional	-----	-----	1 (3.7%)	1 (5.0%)	3 (30.0%)	5 (6.3%)
Supervisor Management	-----	-----	-----	-----	1 (10.0%)	1 (1.3%)
White-Collar	-----	-----	-----	-----	-----	-----
Office Personnel/Staff	-----	-----	-----	-----	1 (10.0%)	1 (1.3%)
Total New Middle:	-----	-----	2 (7.4%)	3 (15.0%)	5 (50.0%)	10 (12.5%)
Skilled Trade	-----	-----	-----	-----	-----	-----
Laborer	-----	-----	-----	1 (5.0%)	-----	1 (1.3%)
Total Blue Collar:	-----	-----	-----	1 (5.0%)	-----	1 (1.3%)
Total, All Simultaneous Occupational Pursuits	7 (100.0%)	16 (100.0%)	27 (100.0%)	20 (100.0%)	10 (100.0%)	80 (100.0%)
Proportion of Total Database Occupations	43.8%	48.5%	27.8%	18.2%	6.9%	20.0%

Even so, most of those pursuing simultaneous occupations were found in the old middle class, even after the transition created by the Industrial Revolution. Indeed, the vast majority were farmers, who comprised two out of three of those with multiple occupations. This is not surprising, for several reasons. First (and especially before the Industrial Revolution), farmers necessarily possessed a variety of skills and abilities related to self-sufficiency. Second, the intensity of much farm work is seasonal. There were significant periods of relative inactivity to which other pursuits could be turned. Third, farms were family enterprises. Large farm families often had a surplus of labor, which could be used to good effect in secondary occupational pursuits.

Aside from farmers, most of the rest of those engaged in multiple occupations were in the upper reaches of the old/new middles class—professionals, business proprietors, executives, and semi-professionals. Those in the lower reaches—skilled trade proprietors, supervisors, white-collar workers, and office personnel—rarely (if ever) pursued two or more occupations at the same time. Individuals in the blue collar ranks virtually always were engaged in a single occupation.

Further insights into simultaneous occupational pursuits may be gained by examination of the secondary positions that were held, as illustrated in Table 5-D.[3] Not unsurprisingly, a significant proportion of secondary concomitant pursuits were in a related profession, entrepreneurship, or skilled trade. Examples abound, such as an attorney and a physician who were each also college professors in their particular fields. A musician and a nurse taught their particular professions at the secondary educational level. Two newspaper publishers were, respectively, a magazine editor and a press secretary. Many farmers were also carpenters, or owned and operated grist or lumber mills.

---

[3]   It should be understood that the secondary occupational pursuit categories in Table 5-D were determined *relative to* an individual's primary occupation, not by the secondary occupation per se. Therefore, for a farmer, a secondary pursuit of teaching was classified as an unrelated profession, while teaching for a minister was categorized as a related occupation. Representative illustrations for all Table 5-D secondary occupational categorizations are found in Appendix H.

Table 5-D. Distribution of Database Secondary Occupational Pursuits Relative to Main Occupation, by Old Middle, New Middle, and Blue Collar Class Categories

Occupational Category	Secondary Occupational Pursuit Category							
	Related profession	Related entrepreneurship	Related trade/ability	Public office/service	Unrelated profession	Unrelated entrepreneurship	Unrelated trade	Total
Professional	7 (50.0%)	----	----	6 (17.1%)	----	----	1 (20.0%)	14 (11.1%)
Proprietor, Farm	----	16 (94.1%)	25 (100.0%)	19 (54.3%)	18 (81.8%)	7 (87.5%)	1 (20.0%)	86 (68.3%)
Proprietor, Business	2 (14.3%)	----	----	8 (22.9%)	3 (13.6%)	1 (12.5%)	1 (20.0%)	15 (11.9%)
Proprietor, Skilled Trade	----	1	----	----	----	----	----	1 (0.8%)
Total Old Middle:	9 (64.3%)	17 (100.0%)	25 (100.0%)	33 (94.3%)	21 (95.5%)	8 (100.0%)	3 (60.0%)	116 (92.1%)
Executive Management	----	----	----	1 (2.9%)	----	----	----	1 (0.8%)
Semi-professional	4 (28.6%)	----	----	1 (2.9%)	1 (4.5%)	----	----	6 (4.8%)
Supervisor Management	1 (7.1%)	----	----	----	----	----	----	1 (0.8%)
White-Collar	----	----	----	----	----	----	----	----
Office Personnel/Staff	----	----	----	----	----	----	1 (20.0%)	1 (0.8%)
Total New Middle:	5 (35.7%)	----	----	2 (5.7%)	1 (4.5%)	----	1 (20.0%)	9 (7.1%)
Skilled Trade	----	----	----	----	----	----	----	----
Laborer	----	----	----	----	----	----	1 (20.0%)	1 (0.8%)
Total Blue Collar:	----	----	----	----	----	----	1 (20.0%)	1 (0.8%)
Total All Occupations	14 (100.0%)	17 (100.0%)	25 (100.0%)	35 (100.0%)	22 (100.0%)	8 (100.0%)	5 (100.0%)	126 (100.0%)

Many old middle class secondary pursuits involved a decided commitment to the community, as evidenced by those who served in public positions of trust. These were typically non-career, but nonetheless important local-level public offices. The list of positions includes justices of the peace, mayors, constables and sheriffs, school board members, postmasters, county commissioners, and the like. Two or three in the group were state legislators. It is likely that this heavy interest and involvement in public affairs stemmed from a deep-felt sense of civic duty, a sentiment especially prominent in agrarian times.

This sense of civic commitment and responsibility also explains the initially surprising number of farmers who were concurrently involved in professions unrelated to agriculture. Usually, these farmers were also teachers (N = 7) or ministers (N = 6). However, from early on farmers were very strong, perhaps ardent, supporters of both education and religion. Further, these professions were not incompatible with the necessities of agrarian time frames. Teaching was seasonal and formal instruction was scheduled to coincide with farm needs. The ministry was practiced on the agrarian day of rest and, further, not unusually involved seasonal circuit riding. To be sure, it must be said that teaching and the ministry were closely related at one time. In many agrarian homes, the only book was the Bible and much home and formal schooling was directly out of it. The "Good Book" was inexorably linked to reading and writing, if only because the Bible was where family records were registered. Not only were many ministers also teachers, the connection between religion and teaching led to the establishment of a multitude of denominationally-supported institutions of higher learning.[4]

A special note must be made about teaching in the 1800s. For most people, average educational levels were typically restricted to not much more than elementary school. Individuals who had earned even a high school diploma were rather rare. In fact, in that day and age, a high school diploma represented sufficient credentials for a teaching career.[5] As, relatively speaking, highly educated individuals, teachers were much respected members of the community and much sought after. In fact, teachers were in such demand that the vocation was often temporarily pursued early in the careers of aspiring professionals, as it provided support funds used to finance further occupational preparation. This is illustrated by several individuals in the database population. Beginning with the third generation, nine persons were teachers early in their occupational lives. After their educations were complete, all went on to well respected careers, as described in Table 5-E.

---

[4]   Case in point, three of the author's kin were college presidents in the late 1800s and early 1900s. All three were ordained Presbyterian ministers.

[5]   The author's grandmother, Clara R. McCormick, graduated from high school in 1906. According to her diploma, which is in the author's possession, she completed high school course work in elocution, English grammar and composition, civic government, English literature, ancient history, mediaeval history, English history, American history, physiology, zoology, geography, algebra, geometry, botany, chemistry, physics, Latin, German, and French. Such a curriculum rivals that of many college programs today. After high school, she completed teacher preparation at a normal school in just a few weeks. She then entered elementary school teaching, remaining in that pursuit until her marriage a few years later.

Table 5-E. Life Work of Database Early-Career Teachers	
Generation 3:	
Individual #1	Newspaper publisher, mercantile proprietor, farmer, magazine editor, county auditor, and fraternal order national secretary
Generation 4:	
Individual #2:	Physician, U.S. Examining Surgeon for Pensions, school board member, and school superintendant
Individual #3:	Attorney, state legislator, and judge
Generation 5:	
Individual #4:	Attorney
Individual #5:	Physician and professor of neurology and psychiatry
Individual #6:	Physician and U.S. Examining Surgeon for Pensions
Individual #7:	Attorney, minister, and college president/chancellor
Generation 6:	
Individual 8:	Attorney, postmaster, assistant U.S. District Attorney, congressman, and judge
Individual #9:	Farmer, postmaster, deputy county auditor, and county clerk of court

Findings:
Female Status and Occupations

The contention that a female's social standing was dependent upon that of her father or, when married, her husband is strongly confirmed by the data. As a rule, the occupational background of women marrying into the family was rarely mentioned. The genealogies making up the database simply assumed that their social positions were that of their husbands. This explains why, in Table 5-F, there are no entries for the first and second generations. A female marrying the apical ancestors comprising these generations merely took on the status of (usually) "farmer's" or "doctor's wife." The remainder of the table depicts the stated occupations of the husbands who married family tree (i.e., consanguine, or blood kin) females. While comprising a much smaller number than that found in the general distribution of database occupations (Table 5-B), the distribution appears to be much the same.[6] This would indicate a predicted tendency for family females to marry "within their station," further confirming the persistence of horizontal intergenerational mobility.

Table 5-F. Generational Distribution of Database Blood Kin Females' Husbands' Occupations, by Old Middle, New Middle, and Blue Collar Class Categories

Occupational Category	Generational Number					Total
	1 and 2	3	4	5	6	
Professional	-----	1 (16.7%)	3 (13.6%)	5 (41.7%	6 (23.1%)	15 (22.7%)
Proprietor, Farm	-----	5 (83.3%)	11 (50.0%)	4 (33.3%)	5 (19.2%)	25 (37.9%)
Proprietor, Business	-----	-----	1 (4.6%)	-----	2 (7.7%)	3 (4.5%)
Proprietor, Skilled Trade	-----	-----	4 (18.2%)	-----	-----	4 (6.1%)
Total Old Middle:	-----	6 (100.0%)	19 (86.4%)	9 (75.0%)	13 (50.0%)	47 (71.2%)
Executive Management	-----	-----	3 (13.6%)	-----	5 (19.2%)	8 (12.1%)
Semi-professional	-----	-----	-----	-----	-----	-----
Supervisor Management	-----	-----	-----	-----	3 (11.5%)	3 (4.5%)
White-Collar	-----	-----	-----	-----	-----	-----
Office Personnel/Staff	-----	-----	-----	-----	-----	-----
Total New Middle:	-----	-----	3 (13.6%)	-----	8 (30.8%)	11 (16.7%)
Skilled Trade	-----	-----	-----	1 (8.3%	3 (11.5%)	4 (6.1%)
Laborer	-----	-----	-----	2 (16.7%)	2 (7.7%)	4 (6.1%)
Total Blue Collar:	-----	-----	-----	3 (25.0%)	5 (19.2%)	8 (12.1%)
Total	-----	6 (100.0%)	22 (100.0%	12 (100.0%)	26 (100.0%)	66 (100.0%)

More insights may be gained by examining the public sector occupations held by the women in the database, which are shown in Table 5-G. It is noted that a woman's husband's occupation is reported in the

---

6   The proportion of professionals in Table 5-F is noticeably higher compared to that in Table 5-B. This might very well be a bias of those compiling family genealogies. Some occupations are more likely to be reported than others. In other words, there would be more family pride in a daughter marrying a physician as opposed to her marrying a stage coach driver.

genealogy sources (Table 5-F) about half again as often as the employment of a woman itself (Table 5-G). Further, female employment in the public sector was exceedingly rare before the Industrial Revolution took hold. Note in the first four generations, only four women held recognized occupational positions. The professional was a midwife, the proprietor (never married) ran the family-owned grist mill, the skilled trade position was occupied by an unmarried seamstress, and the semi-professional was a teacher.

Table 5-G. Generational Distribution of Database Female Occupations, by Old Middle, New Middle, and Blue Collar Class Categories

Occupational Category	Generational Number					Total
	1 and 2	3	4	5	6	
Professional	1 (50.0%)	-----	-----	1 (9.1%)	-----	2 (4.3%)
Proprietor, Farm	-----	-----	-----	-----	-----	-----
Proprietor, Business	1 (50.0%)	-----	-----	-----	-----	1 (2.2%)
Proprietor, Skilled Trade	-----	-----	-----	1 (9.1%)	-----	1 (2.2%)
Total Old Middle:	2 (100.0%)	-----	-----	2 (18.1%)	-----	4 (8.7%)
Executive Management	-----	-----	-----	1 (9.1%)	-----	1 (2.2%)
Semi-professional	-----	-----	1 (100.0%)	5 (45.5%)	18 (58.1%)	24 (52.2%)
Supervisor Management	-----	-----	-----	1 (9.1%)	1 (3.2%)	2 (4.3%)
White-Collar	-----	-----	-----	1 (9.1%)	4 (12.9%)	5 (10.9%)
Office Personnel/Staff	-----	-----	-----	1 (9.1%)	8 (25.8%)	9 (19.6%)
Total New Middle:	-----	-----	1 (100.0%)	9 (81.8%)	31 (100.0%)	41 (89.1%)
Skilled Trade	-----	1 (100.0%)	-----	-----	-----	1 (2.2%)
Laborer	-----	-----	-----	-----	-----	-----
Total Blue Collar:	-----	1 (100.0%)	-----	-----	-----	1 (2.2%)
Total	2 (100.0%)	1 (100.0%)	1 (100.0%)	11 (100.0%)	31 (100.0%)	46 (100.0%)

Females did not really begin to enter the public labor force until the fifth generation, which would have been in the late 1800s. Only two of these fifth/sixth generation women held old middle class positions. One was an unmarried teacher/minister and the other participated in her family's weaving business. Rather, in keeping with changing times, most women in these two generations entered into new middle class occupations. These, though, were mostly positions thought to require "feminine" attributes. Certainly, the largest part of these occupations were lower-level and lower paid positions, which could easily be abandoned should the woman marry and/or start a family. Therefore, the majority of fifth and sixth generation females became semi-professionals, office workers, or had subordinate-level white-collar jobs. The semi-professionals were almost always teachers (N = 16) or nurses (N = 6); the last was a professional actress. The white-collar jobs tended to be in sales. The office workers were typically secretaries, bookkeepers, or office "staff." The one executive was editor of a newspaper's society page and, of the two supervisors, one was a postmistress and the other a dress shop manager.

It must be remarked that the heaviest employment of females occurred with the sixth generation. Clearly, the outside employment of women was rapidly becoming more accepted, but with limitations. Women were permitted, at first, only into subsidiary "helping" positions, as described above. Several of the employed females in the database never married, and had to pursue careers for economic support. Several others gave up careers immediately upon marriage. Data sources explicitly report that at least seven fifth and sixth generation women left their jobs when they married. The epitome of such career sacrifice was the actress, who was a featured player in eleven silent-era films. In 1922, she married, moved to Florida, and started a family (Internet Movie Database 2009; Pershing 1924: 180-1, 383).

Summary and Conclusions

The study tracked social class standings through six generations of genealogical records, beginning in colonial times and ending in the early 1900s. The first three generations, rooted in an agrarian economy, consisted of old middle class farmers, professionals, and small business proprietors.

Beginning with the fourth generation, salaried new middle class positions began to appear. By the sixth generation, about two-thirds of occupations were new middle class. This explosive growth of the new middle class was almost entirely at the expense of farmers, who encompassed three-fourths of the first two generations, but about ten percent of the sixth. This structural transition from the old to the new middle class principally involved horizontal intergenerational mobility. New middle class children of old middle class parents tended to enter managerial, semi-professional, supervisory, or other white-collar careers.

Many in the old middle class, especially farmers, pursued two or more occupations simultaneously. This was particularly true prior to the Industrial Revolution and its concomitant knowledge explosion, which gave impetus to increasing occupational specialization and complexity. Usually, secondary pursuits were in related fields of endeavor, often entailing skills that were part and parcel of an individual's primary occupation. Farmers entering secondary opportunities could take advantage of agrarian seasonality and the labor pool inherent in large families.

Other important secondary pursuits of the old middle class included serving in important local and state level positions of public trust. This indicates a strong sense of community involvement and civic commitment, which were a part of the ethos of the agrarian era. This sense of civic responsibility also explains why so many farmers had simultaneous careers in either the ministry or teaching. Indeed, teachers were in such demand in the 1800s that it was often a temporary avenue for those seeking support for professional career preparation.

In the agrarian old middle class, a female's social standing was that of her husband. The occupation of a woman marrying in to the family tree was never mentioned, while that of a man marrying in frequently was. However, it is noted that blood kin females tended to marry men of equivalent social standing to that of their fathers. This is further support for the notion that most intergenerational mobility is horizontal in nature.

Prior to the Industrial Revolution, women rarely had recognized occupations. When they did, livelihoods were directly related to a family-based business or profession and/or pursued because the woman was unmarried and needed the economic support. It was only when the

Industrial Revolution had an effect on occupational structure that women began to enter the public employment sector in any numbers. Virtually all of these livelihoods were new middle class positions, but usually of a subordinate, support, and relatively low paying variety thought to require "feminine" attributes. Therefore, typical "women's" employment included such jobs as teaching, nursing, and office support jobs. Further, the nature of these jobs permitted many women to abandon their outside employment once they married and started families. Nonetheless, by the early 1900s, the movement toward the entrance of women into the labor force was clearly under way and gaining momentum.

That American class structure has been historically fluid and flexible is borne out by this study. Before the Industrial Revolution, an old middle class prevailed, characterized by male-dominated small entrepreneurship in agriculture, business, and the professions. Life centered on the family enterprise and community welfare, which were intertwined. Toward the end of the 1800s, however, new occupations began to appear, created by burgeoning technological development, the attendant explosion in knowledge, and the development of large-scale bureaucracies. These new occupations, increasingly diverse and specialized, created the so-called new middle class of executives, managers, supervisors, semi-professionals, and other salaried white-collar positions. The structural movement from the old to the new middle class tended to be horizontal. It also rapidly permitted the entry of women into the public sector, initiating, both economically and socially, the changing status of women in society.

REFERENCES

Broom, Leonard and Philip Selznick. 1968. *Sociology* (Fourth Edition). New York: Harper and Row.

Duberman, Lucile. 1976. *Social Inequality: Class and Caste in America.* New York: J. B. Lippencott.

Encyclopedia of Sociology. 1974. Guilford, CN: The Dushkin Publishing Group.

Henslin, James M. 2007. *Sociology: A Down to Earth Approach* (Eighth Edition). Boston: Pearson.

Internet Movie Database. 2009. www.imbd.com/name/nm0675435/.

Martindale, Don. 1960. *American Social Structure.* New York: Appleton-Century-Crofts.

Mayer, Kurt B. and Walter Buckley. 1970. *Class and Society* (Third Edition). New York: Random House.

Mills, C. Wright. 1951. *White Collar.* New York: Oxford.

Pershing, Edgar J. 1924. *The Pershing Family in America.* Philadelphia: George S. Ferguson Co.

Ritzer, George. 1977. *Working: Conflict and Change* (Second Edition). Englewood Cliffs, NJ: Prentice-Hall.

Rossides, Daniel. 1990. *Social Stratification: The American Class System in Comparative Perspective.* Englewood Cliffs, NJ: Prentice-Hall.

Sanderson, Stephan K. 1999. *Macrosociology: An Introduction to Human Societies* (Fourth Edition). New York: Longman.

A FINAL NOTE: SOCIOLOGICAL

IMPLICATIONS

In *The Wealth of Nations*, Adam Smith (1814:114-5) wrote about the value of children in the American agrarian-based economy as follows:

> "Labor there is so well rewarded that a numerous family of children, instead of being a burden, is a source of opulence and prosperity to the parents. The labor of each child before it can leave their house, is computed to be worth a hundred pounds clear gain to them."

The truth of this is borne out by the estate left by the apical ancestor of one of the genealogies comprising the database of these research inquiries. Frederick Pershing emigrated from Alsace to the American colony of Pennsylvania in 1749. Like many immigrants of the day, he was a Redemptioner, that is, an individual who agreed to become an indentured servant upon arrival in return for the cost of his passage. Originally a three-year indenture, the obligation was cancelled by his York County master after eighteen months. During his Redemption period, Frederick was a weaver, and also worked as a wheelwright and carpenter. These trades he continued after he became a freed man. Also during his indenture, Frederick was permitted to marry Maria Weygant, and the couple soon started a family. Having staked a 1768 claim to a 300 acre "tomahawk possession" farm in Westmoreland County just east of Pittsburgh, Frederick and his growing family relocated there in 1769. He and his wife had nine known children who, the chronicle says, helped considerably with the farm and other family enterprises (i.e., a grist mill, as well as pursuit of the skilled trades mentioned above). In 1794, at the age of seventy, Frederick contracted pneumonia and died. Appraisal records filed with Westmoreland County indicate his estate was worth £277, not including the value of the farm itself. For that day and age, this figure represented a considerable sum. According to the genealogy source, it was known "that Frederick brought very little personal property with him to Westmoreland, hence the value of his estate . . . represents the amount of the property he accumulated there" (Pershing 1924:20-97).

Clearly, children were economic assets in America's eighteenth and nineteenth century agrarian economy. But economic advantage was not the only spur to the era's high birth rates. Elevated fertility was the only way to compensate for high mortality rates, which were especially severe among infants and children. It has been said that, in that age, death rates were higher among children than among other age groups, ranging from one out of ten to one out of three depending upon prosperity (Schwartz and Scott 2010:13). The database genealogies are rife with illustrations, as evidenced from the following statements in the Black family tree (S. B. McCormick 1913):

> "Their children numbered six, four dead and two living. Three of the children died in infancy, the other . . . at the age of nine."

> "They had seven children, three of whom died in infancy."

> ". . . seven children, three of whom died in infancy."

Given these statements, it is small wonder that a typically common response to the question of "How many children do you have?" might have been something like, "Eight, five living."

Indeed, the depredations caused by infant and child mortality could be devastating. It was the rare set of parents who did not lose a single child. The toll could be much higher. An antecedent of the author, Samuel Black, and his wife Jane Mansberger Black, had twelve children. Seven of them died before the age of ten at ages nine, four, three, and four in infancy (Mansberger 1979; S. B. McCormick 1913). Another antecedent couple, Isaac and Frances (Truxal) Pershing had fourteen children. Three died of scarlet fever at ages eight, six, and three, all in the same week. At other times, four more of the children died, two in infancy and two at the age of two (Bourne 2005; Pershing 1924:201-202, 397-402). A son of apical ancestors Patrick and Mary Kyle Black had twelve children, of whom seven died between infancy and age ten (S. B. McCormick 1913). The Mansberger (1979:37) source reports a mother dying in childbirth of typhoid fever. Typhoid also took her first three children, ages eight, six, and four. Even those with extensive medical knowledge (or extensive for that day and age) were not immune. The author's great-great grandfather, Dr. James Irwin McCormick, lost his first wife Rachel Black McCormick in childbirth, along with the twins she was delivering. He and his second wife, Margaret Black McCormick, had four children, of whom one died in infancy and another at age five (Jordan 1908:54-6; Mansberger 1979:40-7; S. B. McCormick 1913).

With such horrendous rates of infant and child mortality, it is small wonder that under-enumeration of births occurred, as discussed in Research Inquiries 1 and 4. Babies were simply not counted as persons until they had proved themselves by living. That this attitude affected both personally and officially kept records is evidenced in the chronicle of the Pershings. According to that record, there is a family legend that apical ancestor Frederick Pershing and his wife Maria bore a child, which died as an infant, in perhaps 1753 or 1754. The story was unconfirmed. Certainly, Frederick did not record the birth, as he did other family milestones, in his family Bible (still extant at the time of the genealogy's publication). The legend was deemed so indefinite that it was disregarded in the family history's preparation (Pershing 1924:34).

Certainly, in a social era in which death was difficult to control but births were not, reproduction was a critically important function of the family. High birth rates were needed not just for the economic reasons pointed out by Adam Smith, but also to compensate for a high death rate. This factor was unquestionably a prime (but certainly not the sole) impetus behind strong social pressures to marry and have large families. According to Winch, beginning with Puritan New England, bachelorhood was regarded with suspicion and even penalization, as life in an agrarian economy was difficult for a single man. For women, the alternative to marriage was most likely service as a menial in the household of a relative (1963:190-1).

Findings from the several research inquiries here provide strong evidence for marriage pressures. Virtually all database adults were married; of the very few who never married, the majority clearly had serious health issues, as evidenced by their early deaths. Age at marriage was relatively early for women. Although teen marriages certainly occurred (see footnote, page 8), female median age at first marriage was consistently around twenty-two and a half for most of the 1800s. Males, on average, tended to marry in their mid-to late twenties, when they had become economically self-sufficient enough to begin a family. While childlessness was surprisingly high (about one out of eight married women in the data pool), most infertility was among those marrying later in life, those marrying much older husbands, those marrying widowers with children, and/or those with chronic health problems (often leading to early death). In the event of the death of a spouse, remarriage was normal. Widowers under age fifty, especially those with children, remarried frequently and soon. Second wives were frequently much younger than their husbands, who were clearly marrying for more children and/or care of present children. As an example, S. B. McCormick (1913) lauds one Mary Black who married a widower and "stepped into this family and successfully became the step-mother of five sons. She subsequently had six children herself." Younger widows had a better chance of remarrying than did older widows and/or widows with older children. Aside from fecundity issues, older widows faced unfavorable sex ratios; there simply were not enough available unmarried/widower men who were the same age or older than they were. Indeed, one out of six widows married younger second husbands, no doubt because of an "age restricted" marriage market.

Reproduction was not, of course, the only function of importance to the pre-1900 agrarian family. The family then was pretty much a self-contained unit that raised and taught, protected, and provided for its members (Benokraitis 2005:56; Henslin 2007:25-6). With child rearing, children learned the value of work early on. Before the establishment of schools, children were taught to read and write, usually by their mothers and usually out of the Bible (Pershing 1924:84). Emphasis was placed on becoming ". . . people of character, law-abiding, loyal to country, good citizens, and (being reared) in the fear of God" (S. B. McCormick 1913). Certainly, the Commandment to honor one's father and mother was a decided filial expectation. As an illustration, one of Frederick Pershing's sons, Conrad, enforced strict family discipline (to be fair, it must be added that Conrad Pershing was a circuit-riding Methodist minister, as well as a farmer). A strong opponent of "ardent spirits," he wrote in his will that any of his children who indulged, even after his death, would receive "ten dollars for his or her legacy, and no more" (Pershing 1924:167). As this anecdote shows, clearly, notions of obedience carried into the afterlife. As another example, Conrad's brother Daniel (the author's fourth great-grandfather, and also a circuit-riding Methodist minister), "required strict obedience in his family and did not permit his children to even whistle on the Sabbath day" (Pershing 1924:194).

Without doubt, the pre-1900s family functioned to protect its own in occasions of sickness, infirmity, and old age. In an age when there were no old age homes or Social Security and where physicians and hospitals were few and far between, care of family members in need was a normal expectation. The database genealogies (see Jordan 1908; Mansberger, 1979; S. B. McCormick 1913; Pershing 1924) provide numerous examples of both widowers and widows living out their days with close relatives. Often, it was noted that these individuals suffered from severe infirmities, such as blindness. Usually they went to live with married sons or married daughters and were cared for by that household. In some instances, the final residence of the elderly was with a married brother or sister. Much more rarely, an unmarried child, typically a daughter, would care for her aged parent. For example, after her children had grown, widow Rachel Long Mansperger (the author's fourth great-grandmother) lived with her unmarried daughter Maria, who supported them as a dressmaker (Mansberger 1979:14). A descendant of the Blacks, Maggie Bateman, was an unmarried school teacher who returned home to care for her mother and become her mother's housekeeper (S. B. McCormick 1913). Like as not, though, unmarried adults were also "looked after" by their families, such as the spinster schoolmarm (another Black descendant) who lived with her sister, married to a physician (S. B. McCormick 1913). Nonetheless, as noted earlier, unmarried adult family members were expected to make meaningful contributions to family welfare, either occupationally (e.g., as a dressmaker or a teacher) or as a menial servant assuming responsibility for household tasks.

The most paramount function of the pre-1900 agrarian family was economic, providing the primary foundation for cohesion and stability. The family formed the basic economic unit, a self-sufficient business in which all family members worked together and combined to meet its needs (Benokraitis 2005:56; Schwartz and Scott 2010:13). Division of labor was based principally upon age and sex. Men worked the fields and women were domestic. However, the lines of labor assignment were perhaps not as strictly drawn then as is generally thought. According to Pershing (1924) women assisted in planting and harvesting. Frederick Pershing's wife Maria spun the flax he raised, but he wove the thread into cloth. His daughter Roxanna not only managed the family grist mill but also was an expert with a rifle, providing the family table with game she had brought down. Still, there was a strongly held belief that a woman's place was in the home. As noted in the previous chapter, women simply did not engage in outside employment until after the Industrial Revolution had taken hold. Even then, a woman was expected, as a rule, to return to domestic duties upon marriage.

The paragraph above illustrates another aspect of the agrarian family business. It was often, in fact, usually, multifaceted. Frederick Pershing was not just a farmer, rather, "like most, (he) engaged in several lines of endeavors." He was also a weaver, a cabinet maker, wheelwright, and ran a saw/grist mill (Pershing 1924:80). His son Daniel was a "jack of all trades," working as a farmer, carpenter, weaver, stone mason, circuit-riding Methodist minister, coal mine operator, and book seller (Pershing 1924:183-94). The relatively isolated conditions of nineteenth century rural life made that century's version of multi-tasking an absolute necessity. Again, the entire family was involved in these various ventures. When Daniel was circuit-riding, for example, his sons managed the family enterprises. For families that worked hard and worked as a unit, avenues to success were without doubt available. As asserted by Pershing (1924:27),

> "Then, as now, social position was based upon mentality and means. Where (a person) had mentality he soon acquired lands, and with them the means by which he might assume and maintain such social position as his mentality entitled him to hold."

Even though the nineteenth century farm family was largely self-sufficient, the functions of the family and community were deeply intertwined (Schwartz and Scott 2010:13). It was realized that chances for prosperity, even survival, depended upon high levels of cooperation and reliance on one's neighbors. To illustrate, the author's fourth great grandparents, Capt. John and Rachel Long Mansperger, were moving from York, Pennsylvania, to Ohio in order to take up land accorded to him for his military service in the American Revolution. An elderly man, Capt. Mansperger sickened and died when the family reached the Ludwick farm in Westmoreland County, western Pennsylvania. His wife Rachel and all her children remained and lived at the farm "according to the beautiful hospitality of those days" (S. B. McCormick 1913; Mansberger 1979:14).

As described in the previous research inquiry, members of the agrarian-based old middle class, especially farmers, had a very strong sense of community and civic commitment. For any number of reasons—economic, familial, religious, protective, educational, and social—members of the rural community were dependent upon one another. Much mutual assistance occurred among neighbors, such as log rolling, and barn and house raisings. There were public works projects including, in the early days, the construction of blockhouses for common defense. These, and Sunday church services, were always occasions for socializing (Pershing 1924:86). Indeed, religion and education were prime interests of the community minded, as attested by the number of farmers who were also ministers or teachers, or both. Examples of intense community involvement abound in the database genealogies. A great-grandson of Frederick Pershing, a farmer (born 1835, died 1915) was a church elder, deacon, and Sabbath school teacher who also had an active interest in public matters, holding several township offices. Another farmer descendant held many church layman offices. A third descendant, a farmer and also a teacher, was a "public-spirited man holding several local offices. (His) interest in all public enterprises was marked" (Pershing 1924:105-7, 115). John McCormick, the author's third great-grandfather, was a long-time justice of the peace, as well as a farmer and a tanner. His son Eli, a farmer and businessman, was a teacher and, like his father before him, a justice of the peace. Another son, Dr. James Irwin McCormick (the author's great-great grandfather) was a teacher before becoming a physician. However, he never lost his interest in education, serving a term as a county superintendant of schools, establishing an academy (secondary school), holding a position on the county school board, and, without compensation, preparing youth for college year after year. Dr. McCormick's public service was not limited to education. During the last ten years of his life, he was appointed to the office of Examining Surgeon for Pensions. He also stood for Congress as a candidate of his county (Jordan 1908:52-5).

As the nineteenth century progressed and the Industrial Revolution took increasing hold, all aspects of American society and culture changed. As improvements to food production, sanitation, and medical care occurred, death rates dropped. Because death came under greater control and because children became economic liabilities in an urban industrial economy, birth rates dropped, especially around the turn of the century. The century's fertility decline was due principally to when women ended their childbearing years. Mean age at first birth remained relatively unchanged throughout the 1800s. A woman tended to have her first child in her early twenties. Around the year 1800, however, median age for the birth of a woman's last child was in the late thirties. Indeed, it was not unknown for women to continue bearing children into their forties. By the end of the century, though, median age at the birth of the last child had dropped to around age thirty, cutting the period of effective fertility in half.

Changes in age at marriage took place. Proportions of female teen marriages declined, due at least in part to a long-term, agricultural recession in the late 1800s. Another deterrent to early marriage was the need for more extensive formal education in order to compete for urban-based "female" employment as office support, nurses, or teachers. On the other hand, median age at marriage for males dropped and the proportion of male teen first marriages increased. The salaries and wages of city employment allowed men to acquire the financial ability to marry and start families earlier than was feasible on the farm.

Changing employment patterns engendered significant shifts in class structure. The movement from an old middle class to a new middle class society was rapid, occurring in about two generations. In this relatively brief time, farming fell from the overwhelming majority of occupations to a rather small minority. New middle class positions quickly dominated the occupational scene. The intergenerational mobility creating this movement was largely horizontal. The sons and grandsons of farmers became professionals, semi-professionals, executives, managers, and other white-collar workers. But it was not just males who were undergoing occupational mobility. In agrarian times, females were a part of the family enterprise(s). As the economy changed, though, women increasingly sought employment outside the home. This trend was, not uncoincidentally, just as rapid as the decline in farming as a way of life. True, women entered subordinate, supportive, low paying jobs (e.g., teaching, nursing, office support). Further, women often left these positions for marriage and child raising. Nonetheless, female participation in the labor force was well established by the early 1900s.

The transformation of an agrarian-based to an industrial-based society was historically very swift. Massive changes in social structure, some of which have been explored here, were the result. Nonetheless, the era of free small entrepreneurs comprising the heart of an agricultural society has left us a legacy that is well worth continued examination.

Postscript

The preceding work, based upon analyses of data found in several genealogies available to the author, certainly has its flaws. In the Prologue, mention was made of Dr. S. B. McCormick's comment on the incuriosity of our forefather's toward their ancestry. Therefore, genealogical research has its problems. In compiling the history of his family, Pershing (1924) remarked that the data were as complete as they could be made. He exhausted every known source, but there were cases where no more information was available and others where requests for data were not complied with. Therefore, genealogies cannot be considered an ideal source for historical information and statistics. However, neither can "official" records. Such accounts have been misplaced, destroyed by fires or other catastrophes, or never kept in the first place.

It is argued here that genealogies, in spite of their limitations, can serve as an important source for the examination of historical demographic and social tendencies. Life cycle events recorded scrupulously in family Bibles and later compiled by descendants are probably no less accurate and just as informative as contemporary information that may or may not have been recorded at whatever served as city hall or the county court house. As Pershing stated, quoting a cotemporaneous historian, "Considerably less than half of what we know to a certainty is true" (Pershing 1924:14). Genealogically based studies can provide both reinforcement of and challenges to these "certainties." Either way, future inquiries based upon genealogy sources will add to our knowledge and understanding of the past.

REFERENCES

Benokraitis, Nijole V. 2005. *Marriage and Families: Changes, Choices, and Constraints* (Fifth Edition). Upper Saddle River, NJ: Prentice-Hall.

Bourne, Kathy. 2005. Personal communication (March 21). Ms. Bourne is a descendant of Frederick Pershing through his eldest daughter Elizabeth.

Henslin, James M. 2007. *Sociology: A Down-to-Earth Approach* (Eighth Edition). Boston: Pearson.

Jordan, John W. (ed.). 1908. *A Century and a Half of Pittsburg and Her People.* Vol. III. Pittsburgh: The Lewis Publishing Company.

Mansberger, Faye Lelia. 1979. *Descendants of the Mannsbergs, 1590-1979.* Vol. III. Privately published. Mannsperger Families of America, Inc.

McCormick, Samuel Black. 1913. *Patrick and Mary Kyle Black and Their Descendants.* Pittsburgh: Privately published.

Pershing, Edgar J. 1924. *The Pershing Family in America.* Philadelphia: George S. Ferguson Co.

Schwartz, Mary Ann and Barbara Marliene Scott. 2010. *Marriages and Families: Diversity and Change* (Sixth Edition). Upper Saddle River, NJ: Prentice-Hall.

Smith, Adam. 1814. *The Wealth of Nations.* I. Edinburgh: Oliphant, Waugh, and Innes, as quoted in Robert F. Winch, 1963, *The Modern Family* (Revised Edition). New York: Holt, Rinehart, and Winston, p. 191.

Winch, Robert F. 1963. *The Modern Family* (Revised Edition). New York: Holt, Rinehart, and Winston.

ABOUT THE AUTHOR

Albert E. McCormick, Jr., a native of Pittsburgh, moved to Florida in his early teens. He received a BA from Rollins College, with a major in sociology and a minor in history. His master's and doctoral degrees, both in sociology, were earned, respectively, at the University of New Hampshire and the Florida State University. The bulk of his academic career was spent at a college within the University System of Georgia, from which he retired in 2003 as a full professor. During his last fifteen years there, he served as the chair of that institution's Division of Social Sciences.

After retirement, Al formed M^2 Research and Consulting, through which he has guided college institutions through various reaccreditation issues. He also remains instructionally and professionally active through adjunct teaching appointments, research and publication, and involvement in professional associations. He has been especially active in the Georgia Sociological Association, having held numerous offices in that organization. Its membership twice honored him with its Meritorious Service Award.

During his career, Al's areas of research and interest have included deviant behavior, white collar offenses, criminology, sociology of law, social change, and qualitative/historical methodologies. He has published articles in *Social Problems, Contemporary Crises, Teaching Sociology, Journal of Social Psychology, Deviant Behavior, The American Journal of Economics and Sociology, The Journal of Public and Professional Sociology, Community College Social Science Journal,* and *Journal of the Association for the Improvement of Community College Teaching.* His *American Society: Readings in Social Behavior,* compiled as a supplement for introductory sociology courses, was published in three different editions. Al has also delivered numerous research papers at the meetings of state and regional professional associations.

Al now resides in Florida with his wife and fellow sociologist, Michelle. In addition to golf, travel, and the amenities the area has to offer to retirees, Al and Michelle maintain their participation in sociological endeavors and projects.

APPENDICES

APPENDIX A

Mean Number of Children for Database Women, 1715-1964,
by Woman's Date of Birth (with National Data Comparisons)

Year of Birth	N	Database Women: Average Number of Children	National Data: Completed Family Size*
1715-1814	45	6.49	
1815-1829	59	5.92	
1830-1844	119	5.08	5.4
1845-1859	195	4.40	5.1
1860-1864	98	4.46	4.7
1865-1869	102	3.24	3.8
1870-1874	135	3.45	3.6
1875-1879	157	3.15	3.4
1880-1884	167	3.04	3.3
1885-1889	191	2.92	3.1
1890-1894	47	2.64	2.9
1895-1899	48	2.60	2.7
1900-1904	54	2.30	2.5
1905-1909	60	2.08	2.3
1910-1914	59	2.08	2.4
1915-1919	55	2.24	
1920-1924	76	2.42	
1925-1929	52	3.17	
1930-1934	66	2.98	
1935-1939	67	2.42	
1940-1944	68	2.12	
1945-1949	76	1.74	
1950-1954	69	1.55	
1955-1964	42	1.10	
Total N =	2,103		

* National data derived from several sources by Peterson (1969:508).

APPENDIX B

Mean Age at First Birth, Mean Age at Last Birth, and
Mean Years of Childbearing for Database Women, 1715-1979, by Year of First Birth

Year of First Birth	Mean Age at First Birth		Mean Age at Last Birth		Mean Years of Childbearing
	N	Age	N	Age	
1740-1839	51	21.5	49	35.6	14.1
1840-1849	31	22.5	31	36.5	14.0
1850-1859	59	22.5	58	35.3	12.8
1860-1869	86	23.7	83	35.9	12.2
1870-1874	67	23.2	66	33.4	10.2
1875-1879	69	22.8	68	33.4	10.6
1880-1884	72	23.0	72	34.2	11.2
1885-1889	88	22.6	88	32.1	9.5
1890-1894	104	24.0	102	32.6	8.6
1895-1899	116	23.7	116	31.8	8.1
1900-1904	182	24.1	182	31.4	7.3
1905-1909	194	23.5	57	30.8	7.3
1910-1914	184	23.3	50	30.5	7.2
1915-1919	221	23.2	34	31.1	7.9
1920-1924	146	23.1	38	28.6	5.5
1925-1929	30	23.5	40	29.3	5.8
1930-1934	42	23.8	54	30.3	6.5
1935-1939	40	22.1	49	27.4	5.3
1940-1944	41	23.4	47	31.3	7.9
1945-1949	59	25.0	77	32.0	7.0
1950-1954	50	24.0	67	31.7	7.7
1955-1959	47	22.3	59	28.9	6.6
1960-1964	51	21.9	68	26.0	4.1
1965-1969	46	21.2	63	24.8	3.6
1970-1974	64	21.9	74	25.6	3.7
1975-1979	45	22.1	62	23.5	1.4
Total N =	2,173		1,753		

APPENDIX C

Median Age at First Marriage for Database Males and Females,
1750-1979, by Year of Marriage (with National Data Comparisons)

Year	Database Male N	Database Male Median	National Data Male Median*	Database Female N	Database Female Median	National Data Female Median*
1750-1859	130	25.2		136	21.2	
1860-1874	147	24.8		156	21.7	
1875-1884	165	24.9		163	21.8	
1885-1894	224	25.6	26.1	231	21.8	22.0
1895-1904	348	25.6	25.9	347	22.4	21.9
1905-1914	432	24.6	25.1	437	21.8	21.6
1915-1924	445	24.7	24.6	441	21.9	21.2
1925-1934	57	23.4	24.3	71	21.0	21.3
1935-1944	83	23.8	24.3	90	20.5	21.5
1945-1954	111	22.7	22.8	96	19.9	20.1
1955-1964	94	21.5	22.8	105	19.8	20.3
1965-1969	61	21.8	22.8	57	19.3	20.6
1970-1974	60	22.5	23.2	67	19.8	20.8
1975-1979	52	23.0	24.7	56	20.3	22.0
Total N	2,409			2,453		

* National data from Leslie and Leslie (1977:5), Peterson (1969:530), and Saxton (1993:172).

APPENDIX D

Percent Teenage Marriages for Database Males and Females,
1750-1979, by Year of Marriage

Year	Male N	Male %	Female N	Female %
1750-1859	1	0.8	52	38.2
1860-1874	5	3.4	57	36.5
1875-1884	8	4.8	53	32.5
1885-1894	16	7.1	65	28.1
1895-1904	22	6.3	98	28.2
1905-1914	40	9.3	128	29.3
1915-1924	45	10.1	132	29.9
1925-1934	8	14.0	27	38.0
1935-1944	6	7.2	27	30.0
1945-1954	15	13.5	44	45.8
1955-1964	17	18.1	49	46.7
1965-1969	12	19.7	31	54.4
1970-1974	7	11.7	30	44.8
1975-1979	9	17.3	23	41.1
Total	211		816	

APPENDIX E

Infant (Under Age 1) and Child (Under Age 5) Database Mortality Rates, 1800-1979
(with National Data Comparisons)

Year	Number of Database Births	Database Infant Mortality Rate	Database Child Mortality Rate	National Data Infant Mortality Rate*
1800-1819	107	28.0	9.3	
1820-1849	602	38.2	29.9	
1850-1859	454	48.5	37.4	
1860-1869	633	39.5	39.5	
1870-1879	918	44.7	33.8	
1880-1889	1,075	35.3	32.6	
1890-1899	1,201	44.1	27.5	
1900-1909	1,259	46.1	28.6	
1910-1919	1,427	39.9	21.0	92.8
1920-1929	702	41.3	11.4	69.2
1930-1939	323	15.5	21.7	52.3
1940-1949	377	10.6	15.9	33.7
1950-1959	468	6.4	8.5	23.4
1960-1969	371	18.9	18.9	21.1
1970-1979	272	11.0	11.0	18.5
Total	10,189			

* Approximated from Peterson (1969:550) and Wrong (1977:34).

APPENDIX F

Age-Specific Mortality Rates for Database Individuals Born 1800-1849, by Gender

Age	Males		Females		Combined	
	N	Mortality Rate	N	Mortality Rate	N	Mortality Rate
<1	13	42.6	10	38.8	23	40.9
1- 4	7	23.0	11	42.6	18	32.0
5-14	8	26.2	4	15.5	12	21.3
15-24	8	26.2	10	38.8	18	32.0
25-34	18	59.0	21	81.4	39	69.3
35-44	7	23.0	14	54.3	21	37.3
45-54	27	88.5	14	54.3	41	72.8
55-64	52	170.5	30	116.3	82	145.6
65-74	85	278.7	73	282.9	158	280.6
75-84	66	216.4	58	224.8	124	220.2
85+	14	45.9	13	50.4	27	48.0
Total N	305		258		563	

APPENDIX G

Occupational Categories
(with brief parenthetical categorization criteria)

Professional (contemporary requirement of advanced or graduate-level education):

> Attorney, college professor, geologist, judge, midwife, minister, physician, veterinarian, etc.

Executive Management (higher-level business or government administration):

> Banker, businessman, college administrator, executive, military officer, newspaper editor, state-level official, etc.

Proprietor, Business (owner any type of small business other than skilled trade):

> Contractor, druggist, grocer, insurance business, inventor, merchant, mill owner, real estate business, etc.

Proprietor, Farm: (owner any type of agricultural enterprise):

> Dairyman, farmer, orchard or grove owner, stockman, etc.

Proprietor, Skilled Trade (owner any type of skilled trade business):

> Barber, blacksmith, butcher, cabinet maker, carpenter, dressmaker, plumber, printer, saddle/harness maker, shoemaker, tanner, weaver, wheelwright, etc.

Semi-Professional (contemporary requirement of specialized college-level education or equivalent):

> Accountant, aviator, commercial artist, educator, librarian, movie actress, musician, newsman, nurse, pharmacist, surveyor, teacher, etc.

<u>Supervisor Management</u> (middle-level business or government administration):

> City/county-level supervisory positions (e.g. county auditor or tax assessor, county commissioner or trustee, justice of the peace, mayor, school board member, sheriff, etc.), foreman, middle-level manager, military non-commissioned officer, office manager, postmaster, railroad conductor, school administrator, service manager, superintendant, etc.

<u>White-Collar</u> (contemporary requirement of at least some non-specialized college education):

> Agricultural agent, business representative, county clerk of court, customs officer, deputy county auditor, home economics demonstration agent, insurance investigator, land agent, pension investigator, real estate agent, tax collector, salesman, subway agent, etc.

<u>Office Personnel/Staff</u> (contemporary requirement of high school education for low-level white-collar work):

> Administrative technician, bookkeeper, clerk, key punch operator, office worker, mail carrier, prison guard, secretary, time keeper, train dispatcher, etc.

<u>Skilled Trade</u> (manual occupation requiring an apprenticeship and/or specialized training):

> Beautician, boilermaker, carpenter, foundry worker, machinist, mechanic, plumber, repair technician, etc.

<u>Laborer</u> (manual occupation requiring no apprenticeship and/or specialized training):

> Coal miner, laborer, painter, prospector, railroad worker/flagman, stage coach driver, truck driver, etc.

APPENDIX H

Illustrational Examples of
Secondary Occupational Pursuit Categories

Related Profession/Semi-Profession:

Physician who was also a medical school professor or an attorney who was also a law school professor.

Attorney who was also a district attorney or a municipal judge.

Musician who was also a music teacher.

Minister who was also a teacher.

Newspaper publisher who was also a press secretary.

Related Entrepreneurship:

Farmer who operated lumber or grist mill on property.

Farmer who also operated an orchard or grove.

Related Skilled Trade/Ability:

Farmer who also engaged in a skilled trade, or commercially utilized a farm-related skill, such as weaving, carpentry, stone masonry, blacksmithing, etc.

Public Office/Public Service:

Individual who held elective or appointed local or state (usually part-time) position, such as constable, justice of the peace, school board member, postmaster, state legislator, etc.

Individual who held a part-time service position, such as Sunday school superintendant, national secretary of a fraternal organization, school superintendant, etc.

Unrelated Profession/Semi-Profession:

Farmer who was also a minister, teacher, or engineer.

Mercantile proprietor who was also a magazine editor.

Unrelated Entrepreneurship/Executive:

Physician or farmer who was also a bank president.

Attorney who was also a newspaper publisher.

Teacher who was also a store owner or ran an insurance business.

Unrelated Skilled Trade/Ability:

Engineer who was also a subway agent.

Druggist who was also a house painter.

Railroad worker who was also a prospector.

INDEX OF AUTHORS

W

INDEX OF SUBJECTS